16
MARRIAGES
that made HISTORY

16
MARRIAGES
that made HISTORY

Thank you for your prayers and support of PRI.

Population Research Institute

PO Box 1559 Front Royal, VA 22630--www.pop.org

GERARD CASTILLO

Scepter

English edition, copyright © 2015 by Scepter Publishers, Inc.
P.O. Box 1391
New Rochelle, NY 10802
www.scepterpublishers.org

Cover and text design by Rose Design

ISBN: 978-1-59417-233-5

Printed in the United States of America

Contents

Prologue[*]

Many books have been written about the individual lives of extraordinary individuals, but there are very few about the shared lives of these people in the marriage setting.

It has been said that behind every great man, there is a great woman (and vice versa). Although this is somewhat of a cliché, there is considerable truth in it. Actually it is almost impossible to write a good biography of a married person without taking into account the relationship with his or her spouse, especially when that relationship was faithfully maintained during many years, to the end of the person's life.

In this sense the life of famous men who owe a large part of their success to the hidden and self-sacrificing help of their spouses is very significant. In this book there are a number of examples: G.K. Chesterton, Jacques Maritain, Emperor Charles of Austria, J.R.R. Tolkien, and Baudouin I of Belgium.

This book is the result of research into the stories of a series of extraordinary persons linked to spouses who are also extraordinary. They were chosen with two criteria: being important figures in an historical epoch and having lived a beautiful and meritorious story of conjugal love. Six of these couples were monarchs and four were writers. To them are

* The original Spanish edition of this book featured twenty-one marriages.

added one example each of persons devoted to such activities as craftsmanship, history, politics, and science.

The majority married for love. Several were political marriages or marriages of convenience that were transformed into marriages of love. For example, Louis IX of France and Marguerite of Provence were married without having met each other. In this case a love arose between them that remained alive till death. While it's clear that the process followed here was neither orthodox nor recommended, it does provide us with a lesson: Good will on the part of both partners is always positive and, at times, works "miracles."

The book also has cases of love against the current that survived the tragedy of war or overcame differences of age or personality.

An awareness of a constant history of marriages that are united, faithful, and happy in the midst of great difficulties is a valuable reference for the present-day debate over the institution of marriage. The testimonies gathered cover a very broad spectrum of historical periods from forty years after the birth of Christ until 1960. At the start of each chapter, the date of the couple's wedding is included in parentheses.

I hope that the description of these marriages will help to restore and instill confidence in this natural institution in the face of the many accounts of failed marriages that predominate today.

Chapter 1

❧

AQUILA AND PRISCILLA (AD 40)

Service to the Christian community enriched their marital and family relationship

The little we know of Aquila and Priscilla comes from sacred Scripture. They are mentioned three times with great praise in the Acts of the Apostles (18:2–3, 18, 26) and three times in the Epistles of St. Paul (Rom 16:3; 1 Cor 16:19; 2 Tim 4:19).

Within a few years following the death and resurrection of Christ, the seed of the gospel had spread through many regions of the Roman Empire. In Rome it was accepted by some Jews, among them Aquila and Priscilla, who converted to Christianity sometime around AD 40, after the gospel had been preached by St. Peter and before they met St. Paul. Both Aquila and Priscilla were disciples and collaborators with St. Paul from AD 50, carrying out a very active evangelizing role in the beginnings of the Church.

Aquila was a native of Pontus. He took his name from the Latin, as did many Jews living in the Roman Empire. He was a tent maker who had established his business in Rome, from which he and Priscilla had been expelled by an edict of Emperor Claudius in AD 49. The Roman historian Suetonius says that the edict was a result of disorders in the Jewish community over the question of Christ.

The name Priscilla is a diminutive of Prisca, which is the name that Paul uses in his letters. She was a Roman citizen, and an old tradition claims that she was a relative of Senator Gaius Marius Cornelianus, who provided lodging for St. Peter in Rome. There are also some ancient paintings of St. Peter administering baptism to a girl named Prisca.

Priscilla accompanied her husband on many trips. Her zeal to spread the Gospel made her stand out alongside Aquila. She is mentioned in Scripture seven times by her own name. In four of these places, her name comes before her husband's, which indicates that she was well known for her apostolic activity. She was also a well-educated woman who helped instruct Apollo, a very learned Jewish-Christian.

When they were forced to leave Rome, Priscilla and Aquila moved to Corinth, the capital of Achaia, situated between the Adriatic and Aegean seas. Because of its strategic position between East and West, it was one of the great metropolises of the Roman Empire. It was a religious, shipping, and commercial center.

There the young emigrants had to earn their living among the Greeks, Romans, Africans, Jews, all with different traditions and mentalities. Corinth was a center for textiles and dyeing (especially purple). Thus they were able to establish their tent-making business and had a number of employees.

A few months after arriving at that large cosmopolitan city, they were visited by a traveler from Athens who asked if he could stay at their house. It was Paul of Tarsus who arrived exhausted by the lack of understanding of his apostolic work by the Athenians. Years later he recorded it in this way: "I was with you in weakness, with fear and in much fear and trembling" (1 Cor 2:3). Paul went to Corinth with the intention of beginning a Christian community there.

Aquila and Priscilla were in sync with Paul from the first moment, since they shared, in addition to the Christian faith, the same profession. They joyfully accepted him into their own home and provided him with a job in their workshop. The couple worked intensely with Paul in the spreading of the faith and gathered the converts in their home, to the point that they constituted a small church. Thus began the Church of Corinth, with a missionary team composed of the apostle and a married couple.

Within the city the atmosphere was one of luxury and corruption, with the worship of all kinds of idols, and with bloody spectacles like those in Rome. It was not easy for the Christian life to become rooted there. In addition, Corinth was consecrated to the goddess Aphrodite. Nevertheless, in a few years the Church in Achaia had become one of the most important. In surroundings that seemed deaf to the motions of grace, Crispus, the head of the synagogue, and Erastus, the treasurer of the city, were baptized, along with other important personages, freedmen, artisans, slaves, etc.

Paul later reminded the Corinthians: "Neither the immoral, nor idolaters, nor adulterers, nor homosexuals, nor thieves, nor the greedy, nor drunkards, nor revilers, nor robbers will inherit the kingdom of God. And such were some of you. But you were washed, you were sanctified, you were justified in the name of the Lord Jesus Christ and in the Spirit of our God" (1 Cor 6:9–11).

In AD 52, Paul left Corinth after an extraordinarily successful work of apostolate as well as some misunderstandings, including being expelled from the synagogue. He made his way to Ephesus, accompanied by Aquila and Priscilla. The ship reached the port of Palermo, and the travelers boarded a ship that took them to Ephesus.

Very quickly Paul preached his first sermon to the Jews in the local synagogue. His listeners were so impressed that they asked him to remain and live with them, but he wanted to go to Syria, although he promised to return. Ephesus was the center of the most densely populated region of Asia, and there was an important colony of Hebrews living there. Some of them, who were part of the Diaspora, had received the preaching of John the Baptist.

These disciples of the Baptist had not received the Holy Spirit—and in fact were not even aware of his existence. One of them was Apollos (an abbreviation of Apollonius), an eloquent man, well versed in the Scriptures. One day, Aquila and Priscilla listened to the preaching of Apollos in the synagogue; they were impressed by his messianic discourse, but they detected something lacking in his Christian formation that they proposed to resolve. Apollo accepted their help and asked to be baptized. Later he went to preach to the Church of Corinth.

When St. Paul wrote his first letter to the Corinthians from Ephesus, in addition to his own greetings he also sent those of Aquila and Priscilla, along with the church that gathered in their house.

We know from the letter of St. Paul to the Romans, written around AD 57, that Aquila and Priscilla returned to Rome from Ephesus, and there too, established a church in their house. Paul, in writing to the Romans, said the following: "Greet Prisca and Aquila, my fellow workers in Christ Jesus, who risked their necks for my life, to whom not only I but also all the churches of the Gentiles give thanks; greet also the church in their house" (Rom 16:3–5). The house of Aquila and Priscilla is probably contained in the foundation of the present church of St. Prisca, on the Aventine Hill. In one of the archaeological excavations there, a tablet was found indicating the owner of the house[1]: *"Titulus Santae Priscae."*

Aquila and Priscilla returned to Ephesus. Around AD 67, in his second letter to Timothy, St. Paul sends them greetings there. The Roman Martyrology affirms that the couple died in Asia Minor, although according to tradition, they were martyred in Rome. They are commemorated as saints on July 8.

A Committed Couple

Priscilla and Aquila were an exemplary Christian couple from whom we can learn much about the commitment and self-giving spouses should possess in the service of the kingdom of God. This is how Benedict XVI expressed it: "We honor Aquila and Priscilla as models of a responsible marriage committed to the service of the whole Christian community. And we find in them the model of the Church, the family of God for all times."[2]

Aquila and Priscilla provide us with an extraordinary testimony of lay ministry: that of doing apostolate as a team, as spouses working for an authority of the Church. From their example we can learn many lessons. We see, for example, how this commitment to the Christian community benefited their own spousal community: "The daily sharing of their life prolongs and in some way is sublimated in the assuming of a common responsibility in favor of the Mystical Body of Christ, even if just a little part of it."[3]

---

1. Benedict XVI, Wednesday General Audience, February 2007.

2. Benedict XVI, February 2007 audience.

3. Benedict XVI, February 2007 audience.

This sublimation of the spousal community translates here into a reinforcement of the unity between the spouses and a strengthening thanks to the virtues of the other. Marriage is thus the environment of permanent perfection and a path of holiness. The spouses are sanctified by fulfilling out of love for God, the purposes and duties of their marriage. It is very significant that in the Bible this couple was never mentioned separately. They were always together, both in their spousal life and in their ministry of service to the Church.

Unity of Life

A second lesson is that Aquila and Priscilla expressed their faith with consistency in their family, professional, and missionary life. In addition they taught that the home can and should be transformed into a small evangelizing community, a domestic Church. As Benedict XVI said:

> Not only in the sense that in them must reign the typical Christian love made of altruism and of reciprocal care, but still more in the sense that the whole of family life, based on faith, is called to revolve around the singular lordship of Jesus Christ. Not by chance does Paul compare, in the Letter to the Ephesians, the matrimonial relationship to the spousal communion that happens between Christ and the Church (see Eph 5:25–33).[4]

Aquila and Priscilla show us that every Christian marriage, in addition to manifesting its love and virtues at home in the presence of one's family, should also live it outside of the home, giving witness before many people.

---

4. Benedict XVI, February 7, 2007 general audience.

An Open and Hospitable Christian Home

Aquila and Priscilla are a good example of how we can keep our homes open to God and our neighbor. In addition, through their frequent moves, their home was as mobile as the tents they manufactured.

Let us recall that when the Apostle Paul arrived at Corinth, injured and discouraged by the hostility and misunderstanding of the Athenians, he found himself alone and without employment. Aquila and Priscilla lovingly received him, giving him a safe place to stay and inviting him to work in their shop as a tent maker. For Paul, that house was not a hotel, but a true family home. Under that roof was born a flourishing Christian community. When Aquila and Priscilla heard Apollos preach at the synagogue and saw his limited knowledge of Christian teachings, they affectionately invited him to live in their home for the purpose of completing his formation. "When Priscilla and Aquila heard him, they took him and expounded to him the way of God more accurately" (Acts 18:26).

They recognized that they were the Church, and that it was their responsibility to instruct others. Their efforts contributed decisively to the evangelizing work in the region of Achaia.

Among the early Christians, hospitality was lived to the point of provoking admiration on the part of the Gentiles. This practice has been referred to as "the glory of the home" and "the flower of home life."

The New Testament epistles exhorted believers to live this Christian virtue, especially toward travelers, known or unknown. "Do not neglect to show hospitality to strangers, for thereby some have entertained angels unawares" (Heb 13:2). This referred to the beautiful gesture of Abraham and Sarah, when they prepared a meal for the strangers who came to the entrance to their tent and who later revealed that they were angels.

The capacity of Aquila and Priscilla to receive people was not weakened by their change of residence and country, their frequent trips for professional and apostolic motives, or the resistance and hostility of the persons that they tried to convert.

Chapter 2

❦

PLUTARCH
AND TIMOXENA (CA. AD 66)

A couple's union strengthened over the loss
of their children

Plutarch was a Greek historian, philosopher, moralist, and educator. He was born in the small city of Chaeronea in the Greek region of Boeotia around AD 46. He died in the same city about AD 125.

The Education of Young Plutarch

Plutarch began his studies in his native city, supported by his grandfather Lamprias and his father Nikarchus. He had two brothers, Timon and Lamprias, whom he mentioned frequently in his writings.

He moved to Athens to complete his formation, and became a disciple of the peripatetic philosopher Ammonius Saccas and the rhetorician Emilianus. His broad erudition may have been due in part to his extensive travels.

Plutarch had great influence on important Roman personages—it is believed that one of them was the young Trajan, the future emperor. Among his friends was Lucius

Mestrius Florus, who granted him Roman citizenship. He became a consul under Trajan and procurator of Achaia with Hadrian. Although influenced by Stoic morality, he frequently argued with those of the Stoic school.

His Marriage and Family Life

Plutarch married a young lady named Timoxena, and they became parents of four boys and a girl. A very religious man, he became a priest for life at Delphos after converting to the Oracle in Chaeronea.

He never knew Christianity, but his theories were similar and he soon became considered a Crypto-Christian. Indeed, some important Christian thinkers were nourished by the doctrine contained in his works.

He lived to an advanced age, dedicated to study, the writing of his works and family life, surrounded by his wife, his children, and his brothers, Timon and Lamprias.

Among Plutarch's historical works the most prominent is *Parallel Lives*, which is made up of biographies of Greeks and Romans, exploring the similarities of their characters and concluding with a comparison. The author explains that he was not so much trying to write history as to study the influence of character on individuals. Following a moral criteria, those described appear either as slaves of their passions or as models of virtue.

His extensive works are divided into two parts: *Parallel Lives* and *The Moralia*. Among the latter are works of an ethical character together with others on very diverse subjects, among them marriage and the family.

A Portrait of Plutarch as a Husband and Father

As an author who gave a great deal of advice on married life, how did Plutarch fulfill his own role as a husband?

The letter of sympathy that he wrote to Timoxena gives a good picture of him as a husband and father. He wrote to her on the occasion of the death of their little daughter, also called Timoxena, which occurred in his absence. The messenger sent by his wife did not find him, and he was in Tanagra when he received the news through a granddaughter. Before that daughter, two of their sons had already died, one being their firstborn.

The letter must have been written in the time between receiving the news in Tanagra and his return to his wife in Chaeronea, in hopes that Timoxena would have some consolation before his arrival.

The writing has a spontaneous character, springing from the heart of its author. It was written hurriedly during Plutarch's brief stay in Tanagra. Plutarch expresses the uselessness of words of consolation and the wailing emitted by strangers; the futility of excessive sorrow, the superfluity of external signs of mourning; the balance between the good and bad things of life; consideration of early death as a great good; and the immortality of the soul, which after death returns to its true homeland.

The document reveals that Plutarch is not the "classic" husband and father, characterized more by giving orders than by affection, but a sensitive and tender person who knows how to console his wife, listen to her, and educate his children together with her.

> You know this yourself, you who have reared so many children in partnership with me, all of them brought up at home under our own care. And I know what great

satisfaction lay in this that after four sons the longed-for daughter was born to you, and that she made it possible for me to call her by your name. Our affection for children so young has, furthermore, a poignancy all its own: the delight it gives is quite pure and free from all anger or reproach.[1]

Love includes consoling the loved one. Plutarch excelled in the art of consoling: he invited his wife to have a positive vision, centered on the happy moments of the past, on their good memories:

I do not see my dearest, why these and other things that made us joyful, while she was alive, should now cause us pain and upset us when we think of them. [. . .] Transport yourself with your thoughts, try to return frequently to that time, before this little daughter was born, when we had no reproach against our fortune. Afterward try to unite this time of the present with that time, as if the things that have occurred to us were again the same. [. . .] It is not necessary to erase the memory of those two and a half years, but rather, on the contrary, count them among what is pleasant, for they gave us happiness and joy.[2]

Plutarch also consoled his wife by warning her against any possible invented (or exaggerated) pain, the fruit of an excessive subjectification of what had happened.

If you are suffering because she left without marrying and without children, you can find comfort for yourself in another consideration, of the celebrations that we had the opportunity of taking part in. . . . She, who has left for

1. Plutarch, *Consolatio ad Uxorem.*
2. Plutarch, *Consolatio ad Uxorem.*

a place where there is no sorrow, does not want us to be sad. For, what sorrow can we have for her if she is now in a place where there is no sorrow at all? [. . .] For those who die in infancy it is not customary to make offerings nor celebrate other rites as it is natural to do for the dead, because they have not taken part in anything of the earth nor of the things of the earth. The laws do not permit mourning for persons of that age, on the theory that it is not pious to observe mourning for those who have gone at once to a fortunate and a better and more divine region.[3]

C.S. Lewis wrote about exaggerated sorrow in his book *The Problem of Pain,* which gives clues to unravel the enigma.[4] In it Lewis reflects on his own experience of sorrow upon the death of his wife, Joy. At first he rebelled, until he realized how disordered his sorrowful thoughts were: he was thinking more of himself than of his wife and of God. The passion of sorrow had darkened his mind. Facing his egoism, he changed the order of his thoughts: first God, then his wife, and in third place, himself. He also discovered that when we rely on faith in our moments of greatest suffering, we realize that we are not alone.

In Plutarch's letter to Timoxena, he showed a great admiration for her. He knew how to express the love he professed. Admiration plays a fundamental role both in falling in love and throughout married life. Consistency in the relationship requires that each of the spouses renew their admiration for the other, trying to capture their hidden values. When admiration weakens, one's tolerance for the defects of the other also declines.

---

3. Plutarch, *Consolatio ad Uxorem.*
4. C.S. Lewis, *The Problem of Pain* (San Francisco: Harper One, 2015).

We express admiration for new discoveries, for what we already know, and also for what has been forgotten. For this it is useful to ask oneself: "What was it that made me fall in love with my spouse in the first place?"

Admiration is a source of mutual enrichment. Psychotherapist Nathaniel Branden puts it this way:

> Apart from providing shelter in the storm, admiration enriches us in many ways. In being admired we feel ourselves visible, appreciated, loved, and thus the love that we feel for our spouse is reinforced. In experiencing and expressing admiration, we feel proud of the choice of the person that we have made, we are confirmed in our judgment and strengthened in our perception of love. [5]

Expressing love in an affectionate way is also a key factor in a strong marriage. One has to show one's spouse what one is on the inside, without fear of confiding totally in him or her.

A frequent error is to share only what one has and what one does. It is usually linked to a fear of expressing one's own feelings. Plutarch demonstrated that sharing a life is much more than merely living in the same house.

A Portrait of Timoxena as Wife and Mother

Plutarch's words in that same letter painted a portrait of Timoxena as a wife and mother and were filled with admiration for her: She raised and educated five children with love, dedication, and sacrifice. She nursed Queronte, the youngest of the boys, despite her own resulting discomfort. She

---

5. Nathaniel Branden, *The Psychology of Romantic Love: Romantic Love in an Anti-Romantic Age* (New York: Bantam Books, 1985).

confronted the death of three of her children with serenity, dignity, and prudence. She lived with modesty and simplicity. Plutarch wrote:

> By the modesty of your appearance and the simplicity in your way of life there is no philosopher whom you have not astonished when they have been in your company and in relationship with us, nor has there been any citizen whom your simplicity has not surprised when you have taken part in sacred ceremonies, sacrifices, or theatrical performances. In addition to such, you showed great firmness when you lost the oldest of your sons and again when the good Queron left us behind. How prudently you kept order in the house on an occasion that gave great possibility of disorder! This was the nobility and love of a mother.

Plutarch and Timoxena's Keys to Marital Happiness

Plutarch counseled two former students of his, Pollianus and Eurydice on how to be happy in their marriage. It was an invitation to live positive attitudes and virtues between the spouses that Plutarch himself tried to practice in his own marriage: mutual respect, reciprocal understanding, tolerance, conjugal fidelity, and so on.

In contrast to earlier historical thought, Plutarch centered the whole significance and weight of marriage on a mutually beneficial spiritual relationship between the spouses, not a mere union of bodies and sharing of material goods.

Plutarch saw the function of the wife in a new way: He did not accept the idea of merely relegating the housework to her. Instead Plutarch and Timoxena both participated in philosophical discussions. He felt the husband should encourage the spiritual formation of his wife with the objective that by doing so their matrimonial union would be more lasting and happy.

His conception of marriage increased the rights of the wife but maintained the role of the husband as head of the family, although Plutarch demanded fidelity and understanding toward the wife in part to keep her honest and faithful to her marriage. He also gave a larger role to love in marriage. The institution was not just for the procreation of children but also the basis for developing friendship and harmony.

Here are a few of the ideas taken from his advice for married couples:

> In the beginning, especially, married people ought to be on their guard against disagreements and clashes, for they see that such household vessels as are made of sections joined together are at the outset easily pulled apart by any fortuitous cause, but after a time, when their joints have become set, they can hardly be separated by fire and steel.
>
> The keen love between newly married people that blazes up fiercely as the result of physical attractiveness must not be regarded as enduring or constant, unless, by being centered about character and by gaining a hold upon the rational faculties, it attains a state of vitality.
>
> Plato says that a city is happy and blessed when one seldom hears the words: "This is mine and that is not mine," since the citizens use in common, to the extent possible, those things that are of some importance. With all the more reason those expressions should be rarely used in marriage. If each of the spouses has affection for the things of the other, their ties are mutually reinforced.

Three Essential Behaviors

The various counsels on marriage given by Plutarch suggest three behaviors I consider essential in marital life.

Navigating the Initial Phases of Living Together

The first essential behavior is navigating positively the initial phase of marriage, the "getting to know each other" phase. Contrary to what is ordinarily believed, the first year of married life is not easy. It is not a time of prolonging the "honeymoon," but a period of risk. Newly married couples find themselves needing to adapt to a reality very different from that of engagement. This period confronts them with the challenge of harmonizing many things: their characters, customs, and ways of living; the tasks that have to be carried out in a home; the criteria for making decisions; their roles and plans, and so on. Continuously living together changes things: the idealization proper to engagement disappears; each spouse reveals himself or herself as he or she truly is, without disguise. One thus discovers that the loved one has unexpected defects that make it difficult to live together. At that moment it is fundamental to begin to accept the other as he or she is, and to develop positive attitudes toward living together—above all, understanding and respect. But this apprenticeship is not easy.

Moving from "You" and "Me" to "Us"

The second essential behavior is growing from a mindset of "you" and "me" to one of "us."

In authentic married love there exists a desire for total union between the spouses. This loving desire to form a stable union between two people doesn't cause "you" or "me" to disappear, but instead out of two arises "us." Love does not reside in the lover or in the beloved individually and independently. Love is not a "me" by myself; love exists with "you," making a union of "we." Love is not individual, but interpersonal: it is a shared reality made up of loving and being loved.

Creating an Atmosphere of Joyful Conjugal Love

The third point is knowing how to create an atmosphere of joy in conjugal love. This requires forgetting oneself as well as a certain creativity—for example, asking oneself each day: "What can I do today so that my spouse has a happy day?"

The Married Love of Plutarch and Timoxena

Plutarch has transmitted to us how he understood and lived conjugal love in his book *Erotica*. Written in the form of a dialogue, it belongs to the tradition of philosophical treatises on love. It is a defense of love between a man and a woman in marriage. This book contains two of Plutarch's most important ideas. The first is the need for intimate communication between the couple. They require moments and places to be alone for quiet conversation, where they can get to know each other deeply and have time for mutual contemplation.

The second is the need to be friends as well as spouses. Friendship is a symptom of a mature love. It reinforces the couple's capacity to unite as persons, preserving them from the evils of division, individualism, and isolation. The love of benevolence proper to friendship is a mutual aid for personal growth. Thus each spouse helps to form the other spouse.

Chapter 3

LOUIS IX OF FRANCE AND MARGUERITE OF PROVENCE (1235)

A political marriage that became a marriage of love

The son of a French father and a Spanish mother, Louis IX was born on April 25, 1214. Marguerite of Provence was probably born in 1220. She was the daughter of Raymond Berenger, count of Provence, and his wife, Beatrice of Savoy. Louis was twenty years old and Marguerite about fourteen when they wed.

Louis's mother, Blanche of Castile, owed her position as Louis VIII's wife in part to her name. The French and English kings specified in a peace treaty that the French king's son should marry a Castilian princess. The initial choice for Louis VIII was Blanche's sister Urraca, but the French ambassadors decided that a foreign princess with the name "Urraca" would not be well received in France, so they chose Blanca (Blanche) instead.

When Louis VIII died suddenly in 1226 in his early forties, his twelve-year-old son Louis IX became king, with his mother as regent. Blanche was a very able ruler, but she faced a difficult situation, part of which was the fact that she was a foreigner in France and therefore faced some negative prejudice. Her life had become extraordinarily complicated, she had lost her happiness with the death of her husband, and she was burdened by a heavy task.[1]

Blanche gave her children a strong religious upbringing similar to what she herself had received. She preferred Dominican religious as the teachers of her children.

In the beginning Louis was not the perfect child that some might suppose. He was violent and inclined to please himself. But with his mother's encouragement, he learned to control himself and be more prudent. He became adept at different sports and studied Latin, philosophy, and moral theology. Little by little his mother inculcated the duties proper to his future task as king and instilled in him the ideal of a life of service to God. She frequently told him: "My son, I would rather see you dead than in disgrace with God through mortal sin."

A part of French society accepted and loved the little king, but another sector—barons and ambitious feudal lords—did not take kindly to conferring the regency on Blanche. They said she was a foreigner, surrounded by Spanish servants, and they accused her of educating Louis in a way more proper to a cleric than a prince and soldier. In reaction to this campaign, Blanche advanced the coronation of the young king, as Louis IX, to November 29, 1226.

Blanche of Castile Seeks a Wife for Her Son

On April 5, 1234, Louis reached the age of twenty. Blanche had her son declared "of age," since she felt that he had the maturity needed to govern. On April 25 of that same year,

---

1. See Henry Bordeaux, *San Luis Rey de Francia* (Buenos Aires: Espasa-Calpe, 1951), 90.

she handed over the power she had inherited from her husband. Blanche had reason to feel satisfied: During the eight years of her regency, there was not a single year that was not disturbed by war or some other calamity, but thanks to her discretion, tenacity, intelligence, and strong devotion to the cause of France, Blanche had unified a nation that, at the death of Louis VIII, was threatening to dissolve into disorder and anarchy.[2]

With the permission of her son, Blanche continued to partner with him in his rule, although now on a secondary level. She watched over the political order she had constructed with great effort, especially the unity of the nation and the permanence of the Capetian dynasty.

Louis understood the idea of marriage as a religious ideal. He knew that his mother would choose a wife for him, but he was predisposed to love that woman, whoever she might be, and he hoped that she would be the one who would occupy his heart for life.

Blanche took this choice very seriously, since she feared that her son's future spouse might be someone with ambitions who would take advantage of Louis's goodness. For several years Queen Mother Blanche observed the various marriageable princesses in the different courts of Europe, seeking to choose the one who would be right for her son. What qualities did she require of her daughter-in-law? Beauty was not important; it was enough that she not be repulsively ugly. The most important things were her moral qualities—above all piety—because religion protects a woman's heart and senses.

---

2. See Marcel Brion: *Blanca de Castilla. Madre de San Luis, Rey de Francia* (Barcelona: Editorial Juventud, 1953), 196.

Healthy, strong, capable of giving birth to and educating numerous children: that is what the future queen should be. Love did not have to be taken into account. Blanche herself had not married for love. Affection, esteem, and habit had given her union with Louis VIII that character of quiet satisfaction, making them known as a happy couple.[3]

Blanche chose Marguerite, the oldest daughter of the Count of Provence. Although she was physically less attractive than her sisters—Eleanor, Sanchia, and Beatrice—she possessed many moral virtues and was very pious. Louis accepted her choice and began to secretly initiate negotiations for a political marriage that, with time, was transformed into a marriage of love.

Once the marriage was approved, Louis and Marguerite, each with a retinue of courtiers, met each other for the first time in Sens on May 26, 1235. They liked each other immediately. She loved him in advance, for himself. He loved her in advance, in God.[4]

The Wedding of Louis IX and Marguerite of Provence

The marriage was celebrated on May 27, 1235. Among those invited were many poor and sick people whom Louis habitually cared for. These poor were provided with food and lodging for several days.

The couple spent their first three nights together in prayer, and afterward lived complete continence during certain times: Lent and Advent, on Fridays and Saturdays,

3. Brion, 213.
4. See Bordeaux, 115.

on the vigils of Feast days, and so on.[5] Thanks to that self-control, the original violence of Louis' character was greatly reduced, and he acquired the virtue of patience that is so necessary in conjugal life. The couple had five sons and six daughters in all, and their children brought them both abundant hopes and many sorrows, which they learned to bear together.

Their Years of Married Life

From the beginning Louis was an exemplary husband and father. Marguerite gave him understanding and the stimulus to work tirelessly for his subjects. She was a loving wife, faithful, self-sacrificing, and, on occasions, heroic. We see this in her decision to accompany her husband on his difficult voyages during the Crusades. Marguerite of Provence had another virtue, and not a small one: she put up with her mother-in-law. For fourteen years, she had to suffer the authority of Blanche of Castile, who, even after having given up the regency, continued counseling Louis and working with him in the administration of the kingdom. The intimacy, both personal and political, of mother and son was disagreeable and painful for the young queen. Blanche monopolized the king during the day; the lovers had to be satisfied with the nights.[6]

What was Louis's attitude in the face of the frequent differences between mother-in-law and daughter-in-law? Normally he chose not to intervene, holding himself above those conflicts. He would go off by himself, intensifying his prayers and fasting, thus avoiding any involvement. But

---

5. Bordeaux, 118.
6. Bordeaux, 124.

occasionally he would openly resist Blanche's intrusions into his marriage—for example, when she opposed her son going on the crusade. Louis did not listen to her and took Marguerite with him on his trip.

Louis IX as an Ideal Model of a Christian Monarch

The king worked with boldness and confidence to attain peace with other nations of Europe. He did not hesitate to confront Henry III of England, whom he defeated at Tailebourg in 1242, later signing the Treaty of Paris of 1259. In addition, he brought internal peace to his country, disrupted by the fighting of feudal lords. He governed with wisdom and prudence. He administered justice personally, listening each day to the complaints of the oppressed and helpless. As a committed Christian he combined his governing with a spirit of prayer and penance. His asceticism was praised by both Catholic and secular writers. Voltaire said the following about him: "It is not possible that any other man carried virtue so far."

Louis dedicated himself to frequent, severe mortification and practiced acts of humility, such as washing the feet of beggars and sharing his table with lepers. He defended the Church from its enemies, established many monasteries, and constructed the famous Saint-Chapelle in Paris to preserve a collection of relics.

He was the last European monarch to undertake crusades against the Muslims. In the first of these, he was taken prisoner in Egypt and was freed after paying a ransom. In the second he set up camp in Tunisia, but the expedition failed, and Louis IX died of dysentery close to Cartagena, on August 25, 1270. He had received the last sacraments on the preceding day. He was fifty-six years years old when he died and had been king for forty-four years. He was succeeded by his son, Philip III, also known as Philip the Bold.

His defense of the Christian religion coupled with his reputation for sanctity led to his rapid canonization by Pope Boniface VIII on August 11, 1297, in the Italian Church of St. Francis of Orvieto.

His spiritual testament, a letter of advice to his son, Philip III, says, among other things:

> My first instruction is that you should love the Lord your God with all your heart and all your strength. . . . My son, you should guard yourself from all that you know is displeasing to God, that is, from every mortal sin, in such a way that you are ready to suffer any kind of martyrdom rather than commit a mortal sin. If the Lord has permitted you to have some trial, bear it willingly and with gratitude, considering that it has happened for your good, and that perhaps you well deserved it. If the Lord bestows upon you any kind of prosperity, thank him humbly and see that you become no worse for it, either through vain pride or anything else, because you ought not to oppose God or offend him because of his gifts.
>
> Take part willingly and devoutly at divine services; while you are in church, guard your eyes and do not speak without need, but call devoutly to God with vocal or mental prayer. Be kindhearted to the poor, the unfortunate, and the afflicted. Give them as much help and consolation as you can. Thank God for all the benefits he has bestowed upon you, that you may be worthy to receive greater. Be just to your subjects, swaying neither to right nor left, but holding the line of justice. Always side with the poor rather than with the rich until you are certain of the truth. See that all your subjects live in justice and peace, especially the clergy and religious.

May the three Persons of the Holy Trinity and all the saints protect you from every evil. And may the Lord give you the grace to do his will so that he may be served and honored through you, that in the next life we may together come to see him, love him, and praise him unceasingly. Amen.[7]

A Marriage Unlikely to Succeed

The way in which this marriage came about could be considered a model of how not to do it. Louis and Marguerite did not marry out of love, but for utilitarian reasons. They married without having known each other and, therefore, without having chosen each other. They did not have the advantage of personal contact or an engagement, so they lacked information about whether they were suitable for each other. To this was added the fact that both were very young. Precocious marriages tend to fail because the couple lacks maturity for married life; they often are not ready to carry out the commitment required and are not conscious of their duties toward one another. The fact that both Louis and Marguerite voluntarily accepted the agreement made by their parents for reasons of state—it does not seem that there was any coercion—did not justify the action, nor did it give reason for hope. When looking at their situation, there was, however, one positive factor that could make this political marriage become, with time, a marriage of love. I refer to Louis and Marguerite's personal predisposition to love each other: "They liked each other immediately. She loved him in advance for himself. He loved her in advance in God."[8]

---

7. *Acta Sanctorum* (*Acts of the Saints*), August 5 [1868] 1, 546.

8. Bordeaux, 115.

At first they did not love each other, but they *wanted* to love each other. They did not have feelings of love, but they began by willing to love, and this would be a decisive factor throughout their married life. Canon Law and Natural Law Professor Javier Hervada has explained the importance of this second dimension of love:

> The essential core of married love is not the feeling of affection, nor instinct, nor falling in love: it is the will that gives impulse and order to the different powers of the human being directed to union, according to the demands of Justice and of natural law that are inherent in that union. . . . The force of married love resides in the deciding act of the will, to which spontaneity adds easiness and assistance, but which it cannot take the place of.[9]

In marriage it is not enough to "love each other"; it is also necessary, above all, to want to love each other: The couple must decide to convert their initial attraction for each other into concrete and continual acts of love. Marriages that last are not usually those which place the emphasis on passionate love, but those which focus on a decision to continue loving one another.

A second positive factor in this love story is that both Louis and Marguerite came to love each other because they were persons of virtue. Aristotle said that true love can only exist between virtuous persons. He added that for one who acts in conformity with virtue, loving well is the natural thing, while for those who are not upright it is very difficult.

---

9. Javier Hervada, *Dialogos Sobre el Amor y el Matrimonio* (Pamplona: EUNSA, 1987), 37, 52.

They Grew as a Couple Because They Grew in Virtues

For St. Augustine, virtue is the order *of* love and the order *in* love. Practicing the virtues in married life intensifies a couple's love, insofar as it creates occasions to concretize reciprocal self-giving. In Louis and Marguerite's married life, they both practiced two virtues in particular: understanding and patience. Love implies understanding. The understanding husband knows how to put himself in his wife's place in order to see things as she sees them and to sympathize with her state of mind, and vice versa. An understanding spouse avoids the unrealistic demands that tend to sow conflicts.

Louis felt Marguerite's understanding when he was weighed down by the problems of government, when he was getting ready to undertake a crusade, when he decided to temporarily live complete conjugal abstinence. Marguerite felt Louis's understanding during the occasions of suffering caused by her mother-in-law.

Louis's position in regard to the disputes between mother and daughter-in-law is debatable. If his neutrality had been occasional, one might have interpreted it as a sign of tact and prudence, but by being habitual it led to the loss of autonomy within his marriage. Louis should have made it clear to his mother from the beginning that he was now first a husband and only second a son. One who marries has to learn to free oneself from one's previous role as a son or daughter in a family in order to fully assume the new role of husband or wife. This means changing one's terms of reference: moving from dependence in one's family of origin to the responsibility of founding a family of one's own. One who marries has the right and duty to decide freely with one's spouse their own style of conjugal and family life, and both sets of parents should accept and respect this. Otherwise they make it difficult for the young marriage to develop, and they provoke family conflicts.

In love one has to know how to wait. Patience is an essential ingredient of love and of conjugal happiness. One writer explains it explains it this way:

> True love flourishes little by little; it needs time, some rainfall, tears and daily laughter, some dark hours lived together, successive mutual revelations, weaknesses, forgiveness granted again and again. Disillusionment makes many marriages fail through impatience, through weakness in penetrating into the vital riches of the other spouse.[10]

We've seen how Louis forced himself to control his character, which led him to acquire the virtue of patience. Marguerite exercised patience by putting up with her mother-in-law for fourteen years and waiting for her husband without complaining during his frequent military expeditions.

A Love that Remained Ever Alive

In his analysis of conjugal love, St. Francis de Sales used the example of Louis IX and Marguerite's marriage:

> Their affection resisted the two great obstacles ready to destroy the happiness of spouses: habit, taking each other for granted, and jealousy. For getting used to each other in marriage can give rise to indifference, a patient and sure destruction of married life. . . . A love which does not express itself, which leaves it to the past and the future to

---

10. Juan Bautista Torrello, *Psicologia Abierta* (Madrid: Rialp, 1972), 27.

show its reality, is already very sick. It prepares for those famous crises of the thirties or the forties which novelists have so often written about.[11]

One of the worst and most frequent dangers that threaten married life is routine. With the passage of the years, some married persons become comfortable in their relationship with each other. Every day is the same; there are no novelties or surprises anymore. Love loses its character as a conquest, an adventure. Conversation disappears. As a consequence disillusionment and boredom set in.

To avoid this unhealthy state, each spouse should make an effort to rediscover reasons to continue admiring the other. For example, a wife might ask herself once in a while: "What made me fall in love with my husband?" That which made a couple fall in love remains, but it must be reactivated. It is fundamental to have a permanent attitude of renewal regarding love and marriage, seeing each new day as a fresh adventure.

True love is not repetitive—it is always new and creative; it knows how to invent. But this does not happen by itself; effort must be taken to build it day by day:

> The call of love stays alive because those in love take care each day to bring sufficient wood to keep the fire from going out. The problem is that the wood is further away every day, and each day the effort needed to find it is greater, but there is always wood. One has to want to make the effort to find it![12]

---

11. Bordeaux, 119.

12. Gerardo Castillo, *Confidencias de Casados Famosos y Felices* (Barcelona: Amat, 2007), 207.

A "Second" Love that Surpassed the First

During their thirty-five years of life together, Louis and Marguerite's love not only did not decline—it grew and was enriched. It confirmed once more what we know from tradition:

> Spousal love is a long period of patience which is completed by age. Marriage should not be a descent, but an ascent, but there are no ascents without sacrifice. If they bear together the joys and pains of daily life before God and with the strength of God, then little by little the "second" love will develop, which is the true mystery of marriage. It surpasses the first as maturity surpasses youth, and as the heart that knows how to make renunciations, surpasses that which does not know anything other than to open itself and expand. Something great is produced there, but as the fruit of many sacrifices and renunciations.[13]

Marital love evolves with the passage of the years. This enables it to mature and be perfected, but that accomplishment is not attained without the sacrifice of spouses who together confront the pains and sorrows life brings. That was the attitude of Louis and Marguerite.

The successive stages of married love are doorways to new ways of loving. They are invitations to love more and better. Good love flees from immobility and tends to adapt itself to new circumstances; what is good at one stage may not be so in another. Love that does not evolve, that does not adapt to new situations, is a love that is stalled in immaturity and gives rise to conflicts.

---

13. Bordeaux, 126.

With the passage of the years love tends to be less passionate, but instead is reinforced by friendship between the spouses, bringing with it dialogue, intimacy, understanding, consolation, help, and companionship. Marriage should become richer and deeper as the years go by. Such spouses will ordinarily not find themselves in any crisis. A key factor of mature married love is the shared experience of confronting and overcoming trials. Every trial confronted together unites the spouses more and fortifies their love.

Chapter 4

———— ✦ ————

ELIZABETH OF HUNGARY AND LOUIS OF THURINGIA (1220)

A love that went against the current

E lizabeth was born on July 7, 1207, in the city of Pressburg (Bratislava), on the shores of the Danube, very close to Vienna. It was the ancient holy city of the kings of Hungary, of Roman origin. At that time the Hungarian throne was occupied by her father, Andrew II, a just and charitable monarch who was close to the Church and pious and generous to the poor. He was married to Gertrude of Andechs-Merania, who was a direct descendent of Charlemagne. She was a good spouse and a good mother.

Elizabeth's sister Violante was the wife of Jaime I and aunt of Elizabeth of Portugal. From her earliest years Elizabeth was noted for her piety and for her charity towards the handicapped. She gave the poor that she encountered whatever she had with her at the moment, usually clothing and food.

Far from Pressburg, in the castle of Wartburg in the city of Eisenach, lived the Duke (Landgraf) of Thuringia, Hermann I, a ruler with considerable power among the nobles of Germany. He was greatly admired for his culture, generosity, and piety. He was especially concerned about arranging a good marriage for his oldest son, Louis.

Someone informed Hermann about the holy life of Elizabeth, and since Hermann was also very interested in an alliance with Andrew II, he sent envoys to ask for the betrothal of Elizabeth and Louis. At the time Elizabeth was four years old and Louis eleven.

At that time royal weddings at a very early age were not unusual. These marriages served to assure a political alliance or to avoid conflicts between two countries. And with a certain frequency, what had been planned as a marriage agreed upon by parents turned into a marriage of love.

A cavalcade of some forty riders set off from Wartburg, led by a woman, Bertha of Beindeliben. Her mission was to negotiate the marriage commitment and, if Andrew II agreed, to ask that he permit Elizabeth to live in Thuringia under the care of her future family.

Andrew and Gertrude agreed to both the engagement and to the idea of having Elizabeth live and be educated in Thuringia. The German delegation brought the young princess to the castle of Wartburg where Hermann and his wife, Sophia, awaited them in a festive style. After giving thanks to God for having heard their prayers, they decided to celebrate the engagement in grand style.

The future spouses lived as brother and sister at the Court of Thuringia until they reached the age considered appropriate for marriage at that time, years later.

Life in the Thuringian Court

Duke Hermann chose seven girls of the same age as Elizabeth from among the leading families of his court, including his daughter Agnes, to form a school in his castle. Two years after Elizabeth's arrival in Thuringia, an event occurred with marked her life forever. Her mother, Gertrude, was assassinated in Hungary under unclear circumstances, related to an internal struggle within the kingdom.

Elizabeth concentrated her thoughts and emotions on God. Each day she escaped from the company of her companions to spend several hours praying in the chapel. She gave all the money she received to the poor. She visited the shanties of the most humble without showing repugnance in the face of contagious diseases. She continually mortified her will in small things for love of God. With the passage of the years, she grew in virtue and interior recollection.

Elizabeth's way of life caused both her future mother-in-law and Agnes to feel suspicion and anger toward her; they considered themselves humiliated. The most notable event occurred during a religious ceremony at the church, where all the princesses of Thuringia took part, resplendent in their rich adornments. Elizabeth was wearing a golden crown.

> Suddenly, the eyes of the saint were fixed on the image of our Lord, crowned with thorns. Elizabeth forgot everything: the conventions and rigidity of a court ceremony. She only saw one thing: our Lord crowned with thorns and she herself with a golden crown on her head. And she could not accept this. To the astonishment and indignation of the duchesses, she threw her golden crown on the floor and pressed her forehead on the paving stones, sobbing for the torments of Jesus.[1]

When Hermann died in 1216, Elizabeth suffered growing hostility on the part of his relatives, councilors, and friends.

---

1. N. Gonzalez-Ruiz, *Santa Isabel de Hungria* (Madrid: Accion Catolica Española, 1944), 24–25.

Hermann had always treated her with great understanding and good will, being her only support, so that at his death she felt like an orphan. She could not count on the affection of her father, since not even news arrived from far-off Pressburg. The persecution and injuries she endured at age nine caused her to shed many tears, although she recovered her joy and peace by opening her heart to God.

Elizabeth's enemies plotted to do away with the arranged marriage and return the princess to Hungary. They based it on Elizabeth's supposed state of insanity, shown by the fact that she ate only bread and water, gave her clothes to the poor, and washed contagious sick people. That, according to the accusers, was not proper to a duchess of Thuringia. They tried to influence Louis's attitude, but without success:

> The persecutors did not succeed in anything but in increasing his fidelity and tenderness towards the innocent foreigner. And the more that others hated her for her piety and virtues, the more he felt inclined to defend and love her. And not content with this he took advantage of as many occasions as he could, without offending his mother, to go and console her in secret in her moments of depression and sadness. In this solitude, without any witness other than God, who had blessed that holy union, they spoke of their mutual and discrete love. And the Prince, with persuasive and tender words, tried to calm the wounds that others had caused in that delicate and tender soul, which made that gentle relationship an indescribable and great consolation.[2]

Louis was more in love with Elizabeth each day. When he returned from a trip, he never forgot to bring a gift as

---

2. Count de Montalembert, *Historia de Santa Isabel de Hungría, Duquesa de Turingia*, Vol. I (Barcelona: Librería Religiosa, 1858), 266–267.

a token of love for his promised one. They say that when Elizabeth went out to meet him, he gave her his arm in a loving way while giving her the gift.

On coming of age at eighteen, Louis was knighted, and he prepared to undertake some action that would accredit him in this role. Before leaving on a campaign against Mainz, he confessed to Elizabeth the certainty of his unbreakable love. During his absence Sophia and Agnes's disdain was redoubled, but Elizabeth bore it with great patience. Upon his return, Louis declared publicly his resolution to fulfill as soon as possible the contracted marriage. He added that he would rather lose a mountain of gold than the hand of Elizabeth.

In 1220 Louis became twenty years old and inherited from his father the title of Duke of Thuringia. That is when his marriage to the fourteen-year-old Elizabeth took place. On the day of their wedding, Elizabeth did not appear with the jewels of her new status, saying: "How can I wear such a precious crown in the presence of a King crowned with thorns?"

Six Happy Years

The marital relationship of Louis and Elizabeth was one of a true conjugal love. The chroniclers of that era tell us that Elizabeth was beautiful, cheerful, modest, pious, charitable, prudent, patient, and loyal. She was exemplary as a wife and mother. She was so much in love with Louis that one day she exclaimed: "O my God, if I love my husband so strongly, how much more should I love you?"

Louis admired the virtues of his wife very much. She corresponded by caring for and serving her husband completely. Their greatest happiness was to be together:

> The alliance of their souls was so intimate that they could not bear to be separated from one another even for the

briefest space of time. So that the Duke, when his excursions were short, always brought his beloved Elizabeth with him, who was happy to accompany him.[3]

On more distant expeditions when Elizabeth could not accompany him, Louis always rejected the invitations of false friends to have amorous adventures. In that way the long absences were an occasion of consolidating Elizabeth and Louis's mutual fidelity. When Louis was on one of his trips, Elizabeth redoubled her habitual piety and penance, took care of the poor, and wore very simple clothing. He never saw her dressed that way, however, because she transformed herself in the presence of her husband:

> Her duty as a wife moved her, when she expected the return of Louis, to wear her best clothes and be very concerned for the appearance of her hair, in order to be agreeable to him, to embellish his life, to give him satisfaction and remove any occasion of sin from him. And it would be a mistake to think that this was a painful effort for her. It was a spontaneous manifestation of her sincere love. She was a saint, but a saint who was married and who would fulfill her duties as a wife better than anyone. The love and service that her spouse received were directed to God.[4]

Elizabeth found the presence of God in the poor and those abandoned by society. She provided food every day for some nine hundred poor people at the Wartburg castle. Since the castle was located on a very steep hill (called "Break-knees") that the sick were not able to climb, Elizabeth built a large hospital at the bottom of the hill for them.

---

3. Montalembert, 291–292.
4. Gonzalez-Ruiz, 31.

There she frequently went to feed them with her own hands and make their beds. The six years that Louis and Elizabeth were married were considered by one English writer as "an idyll of enthralling fondness, of mystic ardor, of almost childish happiness, the like of which I do not remember in all I have read of romance or of human experience."

Between the ages of fifteen and twenty, Elizabeth gave birth to a son, Hermann, and two daughters, Sophia and Gertrude. While she was pregnant with Gertrude, Louis was invited by Frederick II, emperor of the Roman Empire, to participate in a crusade. Being a German prince and a Christian, Louis felt that he had no choice but to accept. Elizabeth, however, gave great thought to the advice she should give. On the one hand it seemed very hard for her to accept a separation of this kind—a very dangerous adventure in which her husband could die—but on the other hand, she saw the supernatural meaning of this enterprise:

> On the other side of the balance there was the magical phrase that had thrilled the heart of Europe for more than a century: to rescue the sepulcher of Jesus. That phrase called even more powerfully, if this were possible, to the heart of Elizabeth than to that of Louis. Before that, before the prospect of wresting the most sacred place of Christianity from the hands of unbelievers, what value had life, or other egoistic and earthly considerations? Elizabeth tenderly embraced her husband and counseled him to accept the call of Frederick. With that the door was opened to the very hard trials that God had reserved for her in this life, to make her clearly worthy, to all eyes, of the highest heavenly rewards.[5]

---

5. Gonzalez-Ruiz, 53–54.

Elizabeth's Long and Painful Farewell

On his journey to take part in the Sixth Crusade in 1227, Louis allowed Elizabeth to accompany the cavalcade through the forests to the frontier of the Thuringia territory. When they reached that point, she asked to accompany him for one more day:

> Louis acceded once more, until at the end of that day it was visible to everyone that that interminable farewell which exhausted the heart without satisfying, could not continue, since the separation, in the end, was inevitable. Before the couple separated with a long and tender embrace, Louis showed Elizabeth a ring that he carried and told her that whoever should come to her with that ring should be considered as his personal messenger and she should believe that he spoke the truth. . . . Elizabeth separated from her husband, saw him disappear around a bend in the road and after that was never reunited with him again on this earth.[6]

Expelled from the Castle of Wartburg

In accord with the law of succession, upon the death of Louis, power was passed to Hermann, Elizabeth's son, who being a minor was under his mother's tutelage. But Louis's brothers Conrad and Henry planned to dispossess Elizabeth and her son of their rights, alleging that Elizabeth did not have the capacity to administer the state. They accused her of squandering the state's income by distributing it to the poor. A sentence ordered her to be expelled from the castle

---

6. Gonzalez-Ruiz, 56–57.

with her children, without any goods. In addition the inhabitants of Eisenach were forbidden to help her or take her in.
She was thus condemned to live as a beggar.

Elizabeth was thus forced to flee with her three children.
That same day she went to a church run by the Franciscan
friars and asked them to sing a *Te Deum* in thanksgiving to
God, who she was certain would never abandon her.

Some families in the principality, moved by the suffering of Elizabeth's three children who were cold and hungry,
offered them their home. Elizabeth accepted, paying the
price of living alone. She lived each day on a few pieces of
bread that she earned by spinning thread. She gave herself
with joy to prayer and poverty.

Other people invited her to return to the court of
Hungary, but Elizabeth did not accept. It is said that a
Hungarian noble went to Marburg to visit her. Shocked
to find the daughter of a king spinning thread and dressed
in coarse cloth, he tried to bring her to Hungary, but she
refused. She said that her children, her poor, and the
grave of her husband were in Thuringia, which was why
she wanted to live there for the rest of her life. Elizabeth
also declined the offer of the Bishop of Bamberg that she
marry Frederick II, the Roman emperor, who was highly
attracted by her virtues.

Faithful to Her Husband's Memory

Why did Elizabeth refuse such an important proposal of
marriage? Before Louis went off to the crusade, he and Elizabeth promised each other neither would marry again.

> Elizabeth did not want to return to the pomp of the world,
> nor to have any other husband than our Lord. She guarded

the memory of Louis with the greatest fidelity and not even the temptation of being empress of the Holy Roman Empire could separate her from her resolution.[7]

When the crusade ended successfully, Elizabeth had the consolation of seeing the remains of her husband, borne by nobles of Thuringia. These nobles visited the usurper Henry, demanding the return of Elizabeth to Wartburg with all honors and recognizing the rights of young Hermann as the legitimate heir to the title of Landgrave of Thuringia. Henry agreed to what they demanded, but Elizabeth renounced everything; she only accepted her dowry, which she wanted to use for works of charity.

From that moment on she lived fully the Franciscan ideal of poverty as a member of the Third Order, giving herself to assisting the poor and sick up until the moment of her death on November 17, 1231, in Marburg at the age of twenty-four.

Elizabeth was canonized in 1235 by Pope Gregory I. "The greatest woman of the German Middle Ages" was a woman who followed the path of Christian love as a layperson in her role as wife and mother. Since that time not only martyrs or virgins were elevated to the honor of the altars, but also wives, mothers, and widows. In 1236 her remains were moved to the church of St. Elizabeth of Marburg.

A Utilitarian Love that Became a Romantic Love

From a marriage agreed upon and planned by two sets of parents as a marriage of convenience, one could only expect a utilitarian love based on calculations. Nevertheless,

---

7. Gonzalez-Ruiz, 66.

Elizabeth and Louis's union was transformed, in an unexpected way, into a marriage with true love. The same thing happened, as we have seen, with Louis IX and Marguerite of Provence, but in their case they didn't meet until the day of their wedding.

In arranged marriages such as these, one essential condition was missing: choice. "Love is by its very essence, choice."[8] Unlike what occurs because of a simple but indiscriminate instinct or desire, in love a specific person chooses and is chosen from among many others. That mutual choice is much more than a mutual liking; it is an act of freedom.

Elizabeth and Louis were destined to marry without having any say in the matter, but when a few years had passed, they broke through that script and chose each other. The fact that they knew each other since childhood and lived with one another in Louis's family for ten years was, in spite of the strangeness of the situation, a continual opportunity to have contact and to deepen their knowledge of each other. During this period of mutual contact, the goodness that each discovered in the other was converted into an attractive force which moved the will of both.

This mutual attraction must have been very strong, since, as we know, the loved ones encountered and overcame great obstacles in their relationship. For Elizabeth, at the age of just nine, her political family made life almost impossible; for Louis the image of his betrothed was constantly maligned in an attempt to break the agreed-upon marriage.

These strong obstacles produced an effect contrary to what was sought, since they stimulated and reinforced Louis

---

8. José Ortega y Gasset, *Estudios Sobre el Amor*, (Madrid: Revista de Occidente, 1961), 133.

and Elizabeth's love. Once more the unreasonable opposition of a family to a sentimental relationship of a child, far from putting out the flames of the fire, revived them and gave the relationship an even more romantic character.

The patience and capacity for suffering shown by Elizabeth was admirable, especially during the period when Louis was absent. And no less admirable was the trust that Louis had in Elizabeth, refusing to let himself be influenced by the gossip of his own family. That behavior expressed a practice of human virtue that is essential for love.

One's attention is drawn to the fact that at the age of only sixteen, in full adolescence, Louis had such maturity as a person in love: constancy, fidelity, tenderness, the capacity to console, bringing special gifts on returning from his trips, and the courage to state publicly that he was maintaining his commitment toward his betrothed.

The Secret of a Happy Marriage

The chroniclers of that era agreed that the marriage of Louis and Elizabeth was very happy. Both spouses understood happiness not as a material reality—the possession of things and the enjoyment of sensible pleasures—but as spiritual—the enjoyment of truth, goodness, and beauty. As Thomas Aquinas taught, happiness is the joy or pleasure derived from having attained an objective good, a perfection; therefore, one cannot simply attain it in a spontaneous and direct way.

Elizabeth and Louis's greatest happiness was being together. That came from the fact that their marriage was a lifelong love affair, comparable to that of the best novels. They loved each other with a faithful, generous, patient, lasting, and comprehensive love.

In Elizabeth romantic love was fused with the love of self-giving actualized day by day. Very expressive in this sense is the enthusiastic way she awaited the return of her husband, carefully dressed and groomed to make his life more agreeable. She made poetry and prayer out of her duties as a spouse. She loved her husband through her love of God. In that approach there was no room for routine, that great enemy of married life.

Those who love each other tend to become a single unit. One who is in love maintains at every moment the desire for total union: one is always aware of one's beloved and accompanies him or her physically or spiritually throughout the day.

It is very instructive that Elizabeth accompanied her husband on all the trips she could. The two maintained very clearly that married life is life in common. The custom of traveling together is a preventative measure against conjugal infidelity. Experience tells us that the prolonged solitude of the traveling spouse is a continual risk.

The Tender and Prolonged Embrace in Parting

The union of love cannot be reduced to a simple union of feeling: it is, in addition, a union in being, an identification of the lover with the beloved. Each one is transformed in the other. The model is the matrimonial union in which each spouse sees the other as what he or she really is: a part of oneself. Thus a long separation is experienced as a tearing apart of oneself, an inner emptiness, and a state of loneliness. And in those cases when one feels the separation is going to be definitive, those sentiments are even more intense.

That is what happened when Louis prepared to say farewell to Elizabeth in order to take part in the Sixth Crusade

in 1227. Since both of them felt it was unbearable to separate—thinking it might be forever—they resisted doing it,
especially Elizabeth, who saw to it that the farewell lasted
for several days. Elizabeth's sacrifice in riding through the
woods of Thuringia to accompany her husband was admirable. And the gesture of Louis showing Elizabeth the ring
that would accredit any messenger he would send her was
also touching.

Their farewell ended with a mutual promise not to marry
again if one of them were to die. Elizabeth fulfilled that
promise in spite of living in misery and having the emperor
himself as a would-be suitor. First she was faithful to her
husband, and then she was faithful to his memory.

Chapter 5

❦

ISABELLA OF CASTILE AND FERDINAND OF ARAGON (1469)

A secret romance led to an alliance of politics and of love

John II, King of Castile, became a widower after the death of his first wife, Maria of Aragon. Having a male heir, the future Henry IV, John II arranged for a second marriage, this time to Isabella of Portugal. They were married on July 22,1447. The beauty of the bride was praised by leading poets of the time.

The fruit of this union was a daughter, Isabella, who was named for her mother and for Queen Isabella (or Elizabeth) of Portugal, the founder of an order of cloistered nuns. Two years later a brother, Alfonso, was born. John II died in 1454 and was succeeded by his first son, Henry, who was not a great success as a ruler. His conduct was said to be immoral and, as a result, the nobility became very powerful. John II's widow moved to a country residence, and the new king sent an armed guard there—probably more to control than to protect her.

Until the age of ten, young Isabella grew up in a family environment separated from the royal court and its politics.

Her mother was very concerned about her daughter's education. And although her mother suffered from mental illness, Isabella developed an intense life of piety through her example. The family had a chapel with pontifical permission to have daily Mass celebrated.

From her early years Isabella began to show a deep faith that was nurtured by her grandmother, Isabella de Barcelos, and Fr. Lorenzo, a Franciscan friar. Her teachers included the Provincial of the Franciscans of Castile and an Augustinian priest. The future queen acquired a broad and varied education, studying religion and culture (grammar, music, rhetoric, philosophy) along with training in the rules of protocol.

Isabella Sent to Live at the Court of Henry IV

At age ten Isabella was obliged to leave her mother's house and begin living at the court of her stepbrother, King Henry IV. Being separated from her mother was hard because they were very close. After Isabella became queen she visited her mother regularly until her death in 1496.

The change of environment was difficult, and Isabella lost much of her freedom because she was destined to live as a member of the court. She later referred to the court as a school of evil customs, where she witnessed the "spectacle of royal power being trampled on, of a sovereign incapable of making himself respected and obeyed, of a state given over to factions and reduced to impotence."[1]

Fortunately, she had some contact with her origins. Queen Juana of Portugal, wife of Henry IV, was surrounded

---

1. Joseph Pérez, *Isabel y Fernando: Los Reyes Católicos* (Madrid: Nerea, 1988), 78.

by Portuguese ladies, and thus Isabella was able to hear the language of her mother and grandmother. In the last years of her life in the royal court, she saw the tension that arose from the violent opposition of the nobility.

Henry IV was married twice, first to Blanca of Navarre. This marriage was annulled after twelve years on the grounds of not having been consummated. After this, he married Juana, the sister of Alfonso V, King of Portugal. After seven years the queen gave birth to a daughter, also named Juana, whom the courts recognized as the heir to the throne. Later a rumor arose that the child was not the daughter of the king, but that of a favorite courtier named Beltran de la Cueva, and people began to call her "la Beltraneja." For this reason a sector of the Castilian nobility organized a violent political campaign against the king, which resulted in a manifesto on September 28, 1464, which accused Henry IV of leaving the State in the power of Beltran de la Cueva. It also called on him to disinherit Princess Juana.

The king gave in and disinherited Juana—although not declaring her illegitimate—and recognized his brother Alfonso as heir to the throne. He hoped for a possible marriage between Alfonso and his daughter, but the early death of Alfonso eliminated this possibility.

On July 5, 1465, in a strange ceremony celebrated in Avila, the rebelling nobles dethroned Henry IV in effigy and proclaimed Prince Alfonso as king, who was only eleven years old at the time. In addition they made him the leader of their own group. Alfonso began to act as king and gave his sister Isabella the important town of Medina del Campo. On July 5, 1468, after a short sickness, Alfonso died and was buried in the Franciscan friary of Arevalo. Isabella, very sad, kept her composure and began to show her maturity and political intelligence:

At the age of 17, Isabella had lived long enough to have a clear idea of the meaning of her life. . . . Isabella grew to adulthood through the blows of anxieties and misfortunes. Her father died when she was a small child and she saw her mother dismissed from the court and develop a mental illness, a tragic fate which always alarmed her and which awaited her at another phase of her life. . . . Religion became a consolation and even a refuge from the moment that she reached the age of reason. . . . The degradation of the court and the scandals of Henry; his despising of her mother; loneliness; the lack of resources, bordering on poverty, that the mother and daughter suffered; the shadow of a forced marriage . . . and the danger to her life from that dance of uprisings, change of heirs, abductions, and killings, forced her to mature. It also made her extremely cautious, though not fearful. When she had the opportunity of acceding to power and of exercising it, she did not hesitate.[2]

Isabella Would Not Be Manipulated

After the death of Alfonso, Isabella, who lived in Avila, became heir to the throne of Castile. The nobles who favored her wanted to proclaim her queen. They intended to use her to increase their own power, proposing that she take over her brother's throne, but she opposed this and opted for the line of legitimate succession, obliging them thus to seek an agreement with Henry IV that would avoid a possible civil war. With this she demonstrated a political sense unusual for her age and times.

---

2. Federico Jiménez Losantos, *Los Nuestros: Cien Vidas en la Historia de España* (Barcelona: Planeta, 1999), 121–122.

By the Treaty of Guisando—September 19, 1468—Isabella postponed the title of queen until the death of her brother, and thus restored the royal power to him. For this reason Henry conferred on her the title of Princess of Asturias, the title signifying the heir to the crown. He also recognized her publicly as his heir in place of his daughter Juana, "the Beltraneja."

With this agreement, reconciliation was brought about between Henry IV and Isabella, and peace was reestablished in the kingdom. Isabella would not be forced to marry against her will. In spite of this, her brother Henry tried to force her into marriage with King Alfonso V of Portugal. When she refused, Henry threatened to imprison her.

Isabella's Preference

For six months Isabella maintained a secret decision to marry Ferdinand II of Aragon, in order to prevent a rupture with Henry and to secure the necessary support and the guarantees of her future spouse. She preferred Ferdinand because he was the oldest of her suitors and the one she considered most likely to support her claim to the throne.

Ferdinand was born in 1452 and had become heir to the crown of Aragon upon the death of his brother Carlos in 1461. He grew up among war and other dangers. He was ten years old when a rebellion of Barcelona against his father broke out that led to a ten year civil war, in which he would later take an active part.

He had a good education and was noted for his ability in political maneuvering, which he inherited from his father, King John II of Aragon.

Agents of John II had been working toward a marriage between Ferdinand and Isabella because the king of Aragon was interested in obtaining the help of Castile for his war in Catalonia and for help against the French.

The Marriage of Isabella and Ferdinand

Ferdinand and Isabella had a legal problem regarding the marriage: They were second cousins. They needed a papal bull that would dispense them from that impediment. With the connivance of Pope Alexander VI (Rodrigo Borgia), they received a supposed bull made in 1464 by the previous pope, Pius II, which stated that Ferdinand was permitted to contract marriage with any princess related to him up to the third degree of consanguinity.

A marriage agreement was drawn up, and Ferdinand agreed to work in close collaboration with Isabella. All decisions were to be made in common, and all decrees would bear the name of both the king and queen—although, according to law, she would be the actual monarch. Ferdinand was limited to being the "Prince Consort."

The marriage between Isabella and Ferdinand was celebrated secretly in Valladolid on October 19, 1469, when she was eighteen and he was a year younger. The marriage, which fused the crowns of Castile and Aragon, would be of enormous importance for the unity of Spain. It signified the end of what in the eighth century had been called "the loss of Spain."[3]

Enraged by this marriage performed without his consent and behind his back, Henry IV retracted what was agreed in the Treaty of Guisando, and he designated his daughter Juana as the heiress to the throne of Castile. This would

3. Isabel Del Val, and Julio Valdeón, *Isabel la Católica, Reina de Castilla* (Valladolid: Ámbito, 2004), 99–102.

later give rise to war between two groups: the pro-Isabella group, supported by part of the nobility and the kingdom of Aragon, and that of the partisans of Juana, aided by the kingdom of Portugal.

An Unexpected Queen

Henry IV died in Madrid on December 12, 1474. Isabella received the news while she was alone in Segovia, since Ferdinand was in Aragon helping his father. Isabella did not wait for the return of her husband to make her first decisions. The princess, who had been recognized as heiress of the kingdoms of Castile and Leon in 1468, had herself recognized as queen on December 14, 1974, taking as a basis the Treaty of Guisando.

On December 13, Isabella traveled from the Alcazar of Segovia to the city plaza where a stage had been prepared next to the Church of St. Michael. She came to the ceremony mounted on a horse, decked out and under a canopy, preceded by a knight with his sword drawn and raised, a symbol of the power of the person riding behind him. After swearing by God, by the cross, and by the Gospels that she would be obedient to the commandments of the Holy Church and would exercise good government, she was proclaimed queen by the nobles present, who swore loyalty to her. Then she entered the church to pray. After giving the royal standard to the church, she had a religious office celebrated in memory of the deceased king. When the ceremony ended, she wrote to her husband in Calatayud. She planned it this way, trusting in the surprise factor:

> Isabella took everyone by surprise, beginning with her husband, reduced to the role of prince consort, which he did

not at all appreciate. He had expected a debate with the principal leaders of the kingdom to examine the conditions in which the transmission of powers would be carried out, he expected promises and guarantees on both sides; in summary, he expected a general negotiation. That was precisely what Isabella wanted to prevent: the transmission of the crown was not open to discussion; it could not be the object of any transaction, least of all of compromise: it is accepted or rejected. Isabella presented everyone with a fait accompli and obliged the nobles and cities to decide clearly.[4]

The news was not pleasing to Ferdinand. He was especially unhappy with the gesture of the sword, which clearly expressed Isabella's intention to be the effective queen in her realm. The prince returned to Segovia by forced march with the intention of repairing what had happened. Ferdinand was not satisfied with being a prince consort, despite what had been specified in the agreement of 1469. He alleged that, as the closest male relative to Henry IV, he considered himself his legitimate successor. After strong arguments with Isabella, thanks to the mediation of the Archbishop of Toledo, they drew up the Peace Treaty of Segovia in January of 1475. It was established that Ferdinand would receive the title of king, together with a guarantee of exercising power conjointly with the queen.

Isabella's daring proved to be successful. The supporters of Princess Juana, surprised and disoriented, lost the initiative. The question of whether Princess Juana was the legitimate heiress became secondary; what this group of nobles demanded was that the nobility have the right to participate in the government of the kingdom on a footing of equality

---

4. Pérez, 96.

with the monarch. But the question became complicated when the rebel nobility allied themselves with the Portuguese invader.

The Reign of the "Catholic Kings"

Henry IV's death led to a period of civil war between the partisans of Isabella and those of the daughter of Henry, Juana la Beltraneja, supported by the king of Portugal, Alfonso V. In April of 1475, Alfonso V let Isabella know his intention of marrying Isabella's niece, Princess Juana, and reclaiming for her and for himself the crown of Castile.

With the Portuguese army's crossing of the frontier, the War of Castilian Succession (1475–1480) began. Many cities in Castile supported Isabella. The queen received subsidies from the cities of Medina del Campo and Madrigal to finance the war. Ferdinand skillfully negotiated the assistance of powerful Castilian families, instructed his army in new military techniques, and personally handled the military direction of the war.

Victory in the Battle of Toro, on March 1, 1476, decided the war in favor of Ferdinand and Isabella, and it ended with the Treaty of Alcobendas on September 4, 1479. Juana renounced her right to the throne and withdrew to a convent in Coimbra, Portugal.

Ferdinand inherited the crown of Aragon upon the death of his brother Carlos. He added that crown to those of Castile, Sicily, and Naples. In addition, the dynastic union of Aragon and Castile came about. Ferdinand received the title of Catholic King, granted by the pope, and later this was extended by custom to his wife Isabella.

Ferdinand and Isabella began their rule by pacifying the nobility of the Mediterranean coast and reducing their power.

Various governmental modifications led to a gradual cen-
tralization. The military ability combined with the political
astuteness of King Ferdinand led to the reconquest of Spain
by Christian forces that overtook Granada, the last Muslim
stronghold in 1492. That same year saw the authorization and
financing of the voyage of Christopher Columbus in search of
the Indies, which resulted in the discovery of America.

The final years of the reign of Ferdinand and Isabella
included the family tragedy of the death of both heirs to the
throne, Prince John at the age of nineteen in 1474 and his
sister Isabella four years later.

Queen Isabella died of cancer in 1504 at the age of fifty-
three. During her sickness she asked that Masses for her
health be applied to her soul. She asked for Extreme Unc-
tion and the Viaticum which she received with great piety.
She ordered that there be no great expenses for her funeral,
but that the money instead be given to the poor, and she
asked that her body be dressed in a Franciscan habit. Her
reputation for holiness spread quickly.

After Isabella's death, Princess Juana, her oldest daughter, was heiress to the throne, with Ferdinand as regent. The
ambitions of Philip the Fair, husband of Juana, forced Ferdinand to leave the regency in his hands, although this did not
last long. The death of Philip in 1507 and the insanity of his
daughter Juana forced Ferdinand to take over the regency
for a second time, at the request of Cardinal Cisneros, who
had temporarily taken over the regency.

Ferdinand took Hermana de Foix, niece of Louis XII
of France, as his second wife on October 19, 1505. He was
regent until his death in January 1516. His grandson Carlos
I (later Emperor Charles V) inherited all of his titles.

Before Ferdinand and Isabella there was no Spanish
monarchy, but a collection of small states. They arrived at

the proper time to bring about a unified state,[5] doing away with the problems caused by local struggles between many small independent states of various types dating back to the Middle Ages.

The couple was buried in the Royal Chapel of Granada, together with Juana I and Philip the Fair, in a lavish tomb built by Charles V.

In 1958 the process of beatification of Isabella was begun by the Archdiocese of Valladolid. A great many Spanish and Latin American bishops have expressed their support of this effort.

A Romantic Wedding for a Political Marriage

Fearing that Henry IV would abort their plans for marriage, the engaged couple met secretly in Valladolid. Isabella left Ocaña, where she was being guarded by Juan Pacheco, in the middle of May, under the pretext of visiting the grave of her brother Alfonso in Avila. Her arrival at Valladolid to free herself from the restrictions imposed on her gave rise to an enthusiastic popular welcome.

Ferdinand left Saragossa in an official manner on October 5, 1469, pretending to be headed in the opposite direction. But then he changed direction and his clothing and accompanied by only six persons, disguised as merchants, headed for Castile. They traveled at night and without escort. At an inn he passed himself off as a servant taking care of the horses of those with him. On October 7 they arrived at the town of Burgo de Osma where, mistaken for marauders, they were pelted with stones by the sentries on the walls of the town. After being identified, Ferdinand dressed himself as

---

5. See Pérez, 121–125.

a prince of Aragon. Passing through the town of Dueñas, they entered secretly into Valladolid on October 14, the day on which he met his promised spouse for the first time in the presence of the bishop.

In accord with the commitments received, Ferdinand presented Isabella with a valuable pearl necklace and 20,000 gold coins.

Some chroniclers speak of the general joy aroused by the couple's encounter. The people, tired of the quarrels between the nobles, showed their sympathy for the young prince, capable of taking great risks to marry his promised bride.

The wedding, officiated over by the Archbishop of Toledo, was celebrated with very few guests. After the ceremony the couple, who were already using the title of King and Queen of Sicily, had to take refuge in an isolated part of Castile, fleeing from Henry IV. Historian Louis Suarez says that, although it was not a marriage for love, nevertheless during her whole life Isabella gave the highest example of faithfulness, dedication, and love.

Isabella's Testament and Ferdinand's Letter

In her testament, Isabella gave instructions that her body should be buried next to that of her husband, and that they should sell her portable goods, with the exception that Ferdinand could choose whatever jewels and other things that he wanted so that "seeing them, he might be reminded continually of the singular love that I always had for his lordship."

This declaration of love had a response in the letter that Ferdinand wrote to inform the cities and institutions of the kingdom of the death of the Queen. Here is a passage:

Today, it has pleased our Lord to take to himself the most Serene Queen doña Isabella, my very dear and very beloved wife. And although her death is for me the most difficult burden that could come to me in this life, on the one hand sorrow for her and for what I lost in losing her, and what all these kingdoms have lost, have torn my heart, on the other hand, seeing that she died in such a good way and as Christianly as she lived, it is to hope that our Lord has taken her into his glory. That for her is a greater and more perpetual realm than what she had here, for if it has pleased our Lord to do this, this is reason for us to be conformed to his will and give him thanks for all that he does.[6]

These words express the fact that Ferdinand was coming to love his wife more and more with the passage of the years. The initial relationship, made up of political interests and friendship, continued to evolve until it became a relationship of love. Perhaps being loved by a woman of such great qualities enabled Ferdinand to respond to that love.

---

6. Pérez, 365.

Chapter 6

THOMAS MORE
AND JANE COLT (1505);
ALICE MIDDLETON (1511)

Happy marriage centers on mutual help

n 1532 Thomas More wrote a brief autobiography in the form of an epitaph. Although at that moment, when he was fifty-four years old, he did not imagine he would die as a martyr—which happened three years later—he had the intuition that he was in the last phase of his life. On May 16 of that year, he had resigned his post as Lord Chancellor of the Realm for reasons of conscience, after fourteen years in the service of Henry VIII. Taking advantage of his voluntary retirement from public life, his political and religious enemies, resentful that More had put the brakes on their machinations, organized smear campaigns based on calumny. In response, More conceived the idea of writing an epitaph with the secret intention of responding in a permanent and ingenious way to the unjust attacks he was receiving.

In the "Old Church" in Chelsea, his tomb is still preserved, with the Latin inscription of the epitaph carved into a slab of black marble. The tomb contains only the head of the martyr—the only thing that Margaret, his oldest daughter, was able to save after he was decapitated (which she did by bribing the person who was given the task of throwing it into the Thames River). The epitaph begins thus: "Thomas More, a Londoner born, of no noble family, but of an honest stock. . . ."

His date of birth is not known with certainty, but it was most likely February 7, 1478. He was the second child and first boy of Sir John More, lawyer and judge, by his first wife, Agnes Graunger, who died when Thomas was four. The More family lived on Milk Street, close to Cripplegate.

In 1490 More entered St. Anthony's School, considered the best "grammar school" in London. His teachers considered that because of his great progress in history, rhetoric, Latin, and English, he deserved to be admitted to the Palace of Lambeth, seat of the Archbishop of Canterbury and Lord Chancellor of England, John Morton. For this reason Judge More, accompanied by his son, went to see Morton. Thomas passed the difficult interrogation to which the archbishop subjected him, and soon became his favorite page. The two always understood each other well, due to their similar way of thinking, their open character, and their love of literature. His years of living with the archbishop allowed Thomas to acquire a very solid doctrinal formation, along with a magnificent preparation for his later political career.

> A stay in the house of the Archbishop was in those days the best entryway to public life. There Thomas learned tact and polished manners, and attained that dignity and discretion that later permitted him to deal well with all levels of society and to act with refinement in Parliament and at the royal court.[1]

---

1. Andrés Vázquez de Prada, *Sir Tomás Moro* (Madrid: Rialp, 2004), 44–45.

In 1492, at the age of fourteen, he enrolled in Canterbury College of Oxford University, where the archbishop had obtained a place for him. He studied literature, philosophy, and Greek. He also perfected his rhetoric. His father sent him only enough money for the most necessary expenses, which helped him to use his free time studying in the library rather than indulging in diversions.

Two years later, at the wishes of his father, he left Oxford without graduating, in order to study the fundamentals of law in the New Inn of London, a professional school of law. Being a law student at Lincoln's Inn, he took part in classes at the Furnivall Law School and maintained a friendly relationship with humanists such as Erasmus. During this period he learned French, wrote some poems filled with irony (which gave him a certain amount of notice), and translated books from Latin to English and vice versa.

Years of Doubt in the Spiritual Realm

Between 1499 and 1503 he worked successfully as a lawyer and professor of law. He also lived for some months as a guest in the Carthusian monastery of London, where he had gone because of his spiritual unrest, but without taking any religious vows.

> Thomas participated in Holy Mass and the meditations, readings, and penitential routines of the monks serving God alongside them while pondering the question of whether that was the way of serving God that God had in mind for him, or whether he was called to live in the midst of the world, pursuing a profession and fulfilling social, matrimonial and family responsibilities.[2]

2. Peter Berglar, *Thomas More: A Lonely Voice Against the Power of the State* (New York: Scepter, 2009), 8.

More left the monastery without having resolved a vocational issue that lasted for several more years. During this time of questioning he encountered a book that would be providential in his life: *The City of God* by St. Augustine. During his reading a key question was raised: How can one reach that contempt of the world on which the City of God is based? The answer that he came to was the following: to be "in the world" without being "of the world."

In 1501 he took classes in the Church of St. Laurence based on the book *The City of God*. Three years later, during the reign of Henry VII, he was elected as a member of Parliament for the first time and also appointed judge and deputy prefect for the city of London.

Four years later he translated into English the biography of Giovanni Pico della Mirandola, written by Giovanni's nephew Gianfrancesco. This book had an impact on More because in it he found a solution to the way of life he was seeking to live.

Pico was a humanist who knew the secrets of the classical Greco-Latin world as well as Hebrew and Arabic science. In a public competition celebrated in Rome, he challenged the intellectuals of Italy. This left an indelible mark on Thomas's memory:

> The tremendous impact produced by the example of Pico, as he first translated him into English, never left him. I do not know what books he had with him before his death in the Tower of London; but anyone who has read the commentaries on the psalms of the Italian humanist and his prayers, will see the thread of inspiration that unites them with the Psalter of More and his points of meditation. . . . More learned from Pico that human destiny rises above cultures and civilizations and that the mission

of the lover is to transform the society in which he lives, Christianizing worldly enterprises and reestablishing the lordship of Christ in the universe.[3]

The Decision to Marry

In 1505, at the age of twenty-seven, More felt himself called to marriage, family life, and a commitment to secular life:

> Concentrating again on the serious problem of his interior life, and convinced that his vocation was to be in the world, he saw no better solution than to marry. His departure from bachelorhood was slow and reflexive. He consulted the matter with his spiritual director and dedicated himself to seek solutions on his own, as is generally the case. Shutting himself up in his room he took paper and pen and made an examination of conscience. From that scrutiny there is preserved a poem entitled "Candide, what spouse must you choose." The poem composed in Latin by the reflexive More is directed in an interior monologue to a not very mature More who is sufficiently youthful to commit any sort of foolishness.[4]

As a result of his examination of conscience, he enumerated in writing the qualities that his future wife should have:

> The modesty of a virgin, the cheerfulness of youth, neither frowning nor impudence; one who likes music and books, who does not get hysterical when facing a setback, nor become overly excited in joyous moments. It seems that he

---

3. Vazquez de Prada, 86–87.
4. Vazquez de Prada, 96–99.

found what he was looking for, or with more truth, someone who could gradually change into what he was looking for.[5]

Accepting successive invitations, More frequented the estate of John Colt of Netherhall in the county of Essex. This knight had three daughters of marriage age. Thomas fell in love with the second, but he chose the oldest, Jane, out of delicacy: He wanted to spare her the sorrow and embarrassment of not being preferred as the firstborn.

His marriage to Jane Colt

Thomas and Jane married in 1505. She was seventeen, ten years younger than he. Jane had been raised in the country, together with her parents and brothers and sisters, and although of the nobility, she did not have much education. Thomas preferred this so that he could educate her according to his own criteria. With this in mind he provided her with lessons in literature and music. He expressed his affection by helping her to develop her personality.

During their first year of married life, Jane was homesick for contact with her family and the Essex countryside. She also suffered from having to follow a discipline of studies imposed by her spouse-professor to which she was not accustomed. All of this explains the fact that she was almost continually in tears. Thomas tried to distract her by taking her for excursions throughout the city of London, but since this didn't work, he took her back to her parents home.

More had to learn that to make his young, gentle, fragile wife happy, the right path was not to replace life in a home

---

5. Vazquez de Prada, 97.

with the environment of an academy. He asked the advice of his father-in-law as one with considerable experience of married life, but he was not convinced by the method he suggested: "Exercise your rights and give her a good thrashing." Instead he asked John Colt to speak to his daughter. After that conversation Jane came and found Thomas alone. She told him that she was resolved to change, and that he should forget all that had passed up to that moment. He gave her a kiss and said that all would be well if she was faithful to her resolution. She was, and we can suppose that her husband also became more cautious and more accommodating in his pedagogical zeal, and that he was maturing little by little, eventually becoming an affectionate father to his children.[6]

Thomas and Jane had three daughters: Margaret, Elizabeth, and Cecilia, and a son, John. The marriage was a happy one, as we can see by the fact that many years later, More recalled his deceased wife as his "beloved little wife." She happily dedicated herself fully to her children and the tasks of the home. In addition she was successful in meeting the challenge of her formation and adapting to her husband's way of life.

Their union lasted only six-and-a-half years; Jane died in the summer of 1511 at the age of twenty-three, leaving the young More as a widower with four children between the ages of six and two.

The Second Wedding:
The Marriage to Alice Middleton

What most concerned More in his widowhood was the care and education of his four children who had lost their mother.

---

6. See Berglar, 106.

He was assaulted by the memory of losing his own mother, Agnes Graunger, and he decided to follow the example of his father who married again. This explains how quickly he married again—just five weeks after Jane's death.

Once more Thomas was faced with the challenge of choosing the right spouse. If the first union was guided more by the heart than by the head, on this occasion he did not have any margin for a romantic idyll. He sought an industrious woman with experience in governing a home and educating children.

He chose Alice Middleton, the widow of John Middleton, a London textile merchant. Six years older than Thomas, she lived with a daughter from her first marriage. Alice was an energetic woman of strong character, but Thomas was happy with her, since he knew how to understand and get along with her.

Despite the speed with which he made the decision to marry for a second time, More always seemed very satisfied with his second marriage, to the point that he said he did not know which of his two wives he had loved most. He was always a faithful husband and an exemplary father. He took responsibility for the intellectual, moral, and religious education of his children. He loved family life and fostered prayer together. His house was continually open to all of his family and friends.

A Trusted Friend of Henry VIII

In 1510 More became a member of the first Parliament convoked by Henry VIII. Six years later he wrote the book, *Utopia*, published in Louvaine, in which he analyzed certain social problems of mankind. With it he obtained the recognition of the leading intellectuals of Europe.

He began to work for the king in 1517, became a member of his private council, and was entrusted with diplomatic missions to different countries. After four years he was named Vice-Chancellor of the Treasury and became a member of the nobility. In 1524 his daughter Margaret married William Roper, a biographer and the son of a Kentish gentleman.

In 1524 Thomas acquired some land in the village of Chelsea. He was seeking a quiet place, separated from the bustle of the city where he could contemplate nature and study philosophy. He also wanted a larger house than his house in London, since his second and third daughters were soon to marry and More wished them all to live together. From his new home he began to visit the most needy families, participate in the processions of his parish, and financially support the construction of a chapel.

In 1527 More was consulted for the first time by the king in regard to his "great matter": his intention to obtain a divorce. Henry wanted Cardinal-Chancellor Wolsey to arrange the annulment of his marriage with Catherine of Aragon. But Wolsey failed in his dealings with Rome, something that Henry would not forgive. In 1530 Wolsey was summoned to London to answer various charges but died on his way there.

In 1529 Henry VIII appointed More as Lord Chancellor of England. He was the first layman to hold that position. More resisted the post at first, because he suspected that Henry wanted to use him as an instrument to resolve his "great matter." He finally accepted out of a feeling of responsibility, recognizing it was a moment of political and economic crisis in the country. The ceremony of handing over the Great Seal—symbol of the power of the Chancellor—took place on October 25, 1529.

More Distances Himself from the King

On May 15, 1532, the English clergy definitively submitted to the supremacy of the king over the Church. The next day, not wanting to support Henry VIII's project, More resigned from his post as Lord-Chancellor. He retired from public life, accepting a new life of poverty and abandonment by many of those he had considered his friends. At this time he wrote his epitaph in Latin and his letter to John Frith in defense of the Holy Eucharist.

On January 25, 1533, Henry married Anne Boleyn, who was crowned queen on June 1. More did not attend the coronation ceremony. In January 1534 More was accused of having written against an official document published with the consent of the king and his council: the Thirty-Nine Articles which contained Anglican thought on divorce and the Church. The book included the threat of appealing to a council against the pope whom it accused of heresy and illegitimate authority. On March 6, More was interrogated before a Commission of the Royal Council. Two weeks later Pope Clement VII declared that the first marriage of Henry was the only valid one.

On March 30 the Act of Succession was promulgated, which transferred succession to the throne to the children of the marriage of the king with Anne Boleyn. Shortly afterward it was added that the marriage with Catherine of Aragon had been invalid. Henry VIII was considered head of the Anglican Church as a reality independent of the Roman Catholic Church, and anyone opposed to the Act was considered guilty of high treason.

On April 13, More and Bishop John Fisher were cited to appear at Lambeth Palace, where they were encouraged to take an oath upholding the law of succession. The formula of the oath was preceded by a preamble in which the marriage with Catherine of Aragon was declared null and the supremacy of the pope over the Church of England was rejected. Before the lords, both refused to take the oath because of the preamble attached to it.

Imprisonment and Death in the Tower of London

More refused to take the oath a second time. They asked him to express his reasons, but he maintained a prudent silence. As a lawyer he knew that if he spoke, he would be sentencing himself to death. And as a believer who meditated daily on the passion of Our Lord, he recalled that Jesus maintained silence before his accusers. He wanted it to remain clear that, being innocent before the law, he was dying for exclusively religious reasons.

His refusal led to his imprisonment in the Tower of London on April 17, 1534. He remained silent until the moment when he was condemned through a false testimony; he then gave an eloquent defense of the indissolubility of marriage and the freedom of the Church from control by the state.

In the beginning he was forbidden to have any visitors and was kept in a humid, uncomfortable cell. He was sick but at peace in his heart. The prayer and faith that had guided his whole life now sustained him. He trusted in God, who never abandons his servants.

After a month had passed, his eldest daughter Margaret received permission to see him. She asked him to give up his refusal to take the oath since the law had been approved by Parliament. More answered that he was ready to lose everything—goods, land, even life—before going against his conscience and putting his soul at risk.

A few months later his wife was permitted to visit him. Cromwell thought that Alice Middleton might be a good ally to get More to give in. She took up the question without preambles:

> My God, Master More! . . . I am surprised to see you, whom until now I had held to be wise, turned into a nit-wit, stuck in this cramped, dirty prison; that you should be happy to be locked up with mice and rats, whereas you could be at liberty and enjoying the King's mercy and counsel. It would suffice if you were willing to do like all the bishops and most cultured men in the country have done! In Chelsea you have a beautiful house, your own study, garden, and your own orchard, and all the other comforts, where you could be happy in the company of your wife, your children, and your servants. I am aston-ished at why, for the love of God, you so stupidly choose to remain in this place.[7]

Thomas listened to his wife with his usual patience. Then he dialogued with her:

> "But my good woman, for God's sake, I beg you to tell me one thing only . . . is this dwelling-place as near to Heaven as mine is?" to which she, who was not at all pleased to hear those words, only replied in her usual rough and ready man-ner: "Tilly vally, tilly vally" [which meant something akin to "silly nonsense" or "rubbish"]. "What do you say, madam Alice," he remarked "is it not so?" "*Bone Deus, bone Deus*, husband, is there no end to all this?" "Woman, if that were so, I do not see any reason to feel happy about my beautiful

---

7. Berglar, 109.

house and everything that goes with it; for if I were to return to it seven years after I am buried, I were sure to find someone else living there who would turn me out saying that I had no business there. So you see, what reason is there for me to have feelings for a house that can so soon forget its master?"[8]

Alice loved her husband to the end. She financed at great sacrifice the expenses of his stay in the Tower and morally shared his martyrdom, but, as was the case with his daughters, she never understood his refusal to swear to the Act of Succession. This last was an added sorrow for Thomas. He regretted the separation from his family, yet he knew himself to be protected by God. And he took advantage of his time alone to think and write.

Among his writings in prison, outstanding were his *Treatise on the Passion of Christ*, *The Agony of Christ*, and *Dialogue of Consolation in Tribulation*. Vázquez de Prada says the following about the last of these:

It has a great deal of autobiography and of contemporary history. It includes, in addition, an eternal value of symbol and doctrine. It is an ascetical book, written by a humanist, that points out to us the norms for living with Christ in times of persecution and apostasy. It is a book of the Church of Silence. And it retains, unfortunately, its timeliness in all centuries.[9]

The prisoner was allowed for a period to attend Mass in the Tower chapel and frequent the sacraments. He used these opportunities to prepare his soul, and during his prayer time he made great use of the psalms.

---

8. Berglar, 109.
9. Vazquez de Prada, 325.

He spent fifteen months in the Tower of London, always maintaining his serenity. During this time he was able to exchange some letters with his daughter Margaret. In one of them he said the following: "I am really as well here as in my own home, because God, who made me a mischievous child, holds me against his heart and caresses me like a little one."[10]

In 1535 the material situation of the More family was dire, since a new law deprived them of the material goods and the rents they had been receiving. Because of this, Alice Middleton wrote a letter to the king that was not answered. The family's goods were confiscated and given to others. On May 4, Margaret visited her father for the last time. Together they watched as the first Carthusian martyrs were led to the scaffold for refusing to take the oath of succession.

On June 22 the execution of Bishop John Fisher took place. On July 1, Thomas More's trial was begun in Westminster Hall. Through a false declaration of Richard Rich, given under oath, he was condemned to death for "high treason." The king commuted the usual sentence—to be hung, drawn, and quartered—to the less horrendous death by beheading.

On July 6, More's friend Sir Thomas Pope visited him very early to announce that, in accord with a message from the king and council, More was to be executed before nine o'clock. As the messenger broke down in tears, More consoled him with these words: "Let not your spirits be cast down, for I hope we shall see one another in a better place, where we shall be free to live and love in eternal bliss."[11]

More walked to the place of execution. On the way he asked the people there to pray for him and declared that he

---

10. Vazquez de Prada, 325–326.
11. Vazquez de Prada, 325–326.

was dying for the Catholic Church. After climbing up to the scaffold, he recited Psalm 50: "Have mercy on me, O Lord, according to your great mercy. Lord, you will not despise a contrite and humble heart." Then he embraced and encouraged the executioner, and his eyes were blindfolded. His head was severed at the first blow. It was exposed for a time on the London Bridge, until his daughter Margaret was able to rescue it and deposit it in the family tomb, located in the Church of St. Dunstan. The decapitation of Thomas More was the culmination of a long martyrdom:

> It consisted not only of prison and death, but also of fear: fear of suffering, fear of being weak, fear of ending up offending God. . . . The martyrdom also consisted, and perhaps in a more painful way, in that he was continually tempted, again and again, in a dangerously subtle manner, since the tempter made use even of the mouth of the persons most dear to him, for example of his daughter Margaret, with the reproach that he was being arrogant, immodest, proud.[12]

On December 29, 1886, John Fisher and Thomas More were beatified by Pope Leo XIII, and on May 19, 1935, they were canonized by Pope Pius XI. If he had not been a martyr, More would have merited canonization as a confessor. In 2000, St. John Paul II proclaimed Thomas More the patron saint of rulers and of politicians.

■ ■ ■

---

12. William Roper, *The Life of Sir Thomas More* (Springfield, Ill.: Templegate Publishers, 1980).

More Discovers His Vocation to Marriage

As noted earlier More "felt himself called to marriage, to family life and to a commitment to secular life." He considered marriage not as an option, but as a vocation, one that was human and supernatural at the same time.

When one speaks of "marriage," one alludes to the alliance by which a man and woman establish a partnership for life. When one speaks of "Christian marriage," one alludes to the alliance of love between the spouses and of both with God: "For a Christian, marriage is not just a social institution, much less a mere remedy for human weakness. It is a real supernatural calling."[13]

The supernatural vocation opens up a whole road of sanctity. More knew that married people sanctify themselves by fulfilling perfectly the duties of marriage.

To respond to the call he had received, More took on the task of choosing a wife with prudence and responsibility. It was to be a decision not based on sentimental criteria but on a prolonged reflection. He wanted to act with both head and heart. He chose a life companion that would have certain specific personal qualities: she should possess the virtues of cheerfulness and modesty, along with the maturity of character that leads to self-control and strength of soul.

More was able to elevate his point of view at the moment of choosing a wife, even though he might be asking the impossible. Very suggestive in this sense is the commentary of Vázquez de Prada: "He wanted a white blackbird. It seemed as though he had found it, but it would be truer to say that he was changing its plumage." Jane Colt

---

13. St. Josemaría Escrivá, *Christ Is Passing By* (New York: Scepter, 1974), no. 23.

made Thomas happy when she began to forget her maiden stage—the old plumage—to accept her new role as a married woman, where attention to their newly founded family began to prevail over her family of origin.

A Happy Marriage Between Two Very Unequal Persons

The initial stage of life in common presents the newly married with the challenge of living together in a positive way, adapting themselves to a different way of being and all the customs of the other. Some differences are already discovered during courtship, but do not present problems because the time of being together is relatively short. By contrast, over the course of married life together, those differences become more present and new ones may be unveiled.

What is advisable in this situation? It is not a matter of seeking a mere "peaceful coexistence" or striking a balance between differences; nor does it make sense to try to ignore or erase them. The most realistic and sensible approach is to synchronize them as one harmonizes the different sounds of a musical piece. One has to assume that the other is different and learn to live with those differences.

In the case of Thomas and Jane, conjugal life initially was difficult, first of all, because of their age difference. Jane was an adolescent of seventeen who married an adult of twenty-seven. To this was added the considerable difference in their education: a girl with primary school studies united to a great humanist. Then there were the differences in their social environments: Thomas was born and raised in a city, while Jane had grown up in the country.

More's way of dealing with the intellectual and cultural inequality was to turn his home into an academy. He thus created an authoritative relationship more like that of a father to a child or a professor to a student than a marriage relationship.

More did this with the best of intentions: to develop Jane's personality and give her access to culture during a period when women had far less opportunities than men. But his method did not have the results intended. Jane did not take well to being molded by her husband, because it impeded her autonomy and personal realization. It was also painful for her to submit to a discipline of study for which she was not prepared.

Another of More's mistakes was not realizing how being far removed from family and familiar surroundings affected Jane. He lacked the ability to put himself in her place, but he rectified this mistake when he accompanied his wife to her parents' home in the country, and he finally developed patience and understanding that allowed their marriage to flourish.

Jane's attitudes also changed and matured. She took up her studies and was happy dedicating herself to her husband and her children.

A Second Marriage Out of Love for His Children

After becoming a widower, More could have taken a year or longer before marrying again. And in that case, he could have waited to fall in love. It would have been normal for a person of his status. But it didn't happen like that: he married five weeks after his wife died, and probably not the woman he would have most liked. Why such a rush in something of such importance?

The answer is that he married out of love for his four small children, in order that as soon as possible they might be well cared for by a mother. More chose a *mother* rather than a *wife.* He wanted the one he married to possess the qualities of a good mother. He chose with his head, not his heart. He wanted a mature woman with experience in being a mother and managing a household. For that reason he accepted a widow older than himself, as well as a child from her previous marriage. More thus sacrificed his personal welfare for the happiness of his children, which proved that he was a good father, and showed his great vision of marriage:

> He had a very practical idea of marriage as a sacrament and of the institution of the family. The education of the children, the affection of the spouses, and the economy of the home were above the subjective refinements of love. . . . He considered marriage as a state which permitted him to remain in the world and continue forward with his plan of spiritual perfection as a means of sanctifying persons and domestic duties.[14]

The secret of success for this second marriage was that he treated Alice Middleton with love, gentleness, patience, perseverance, and a sense of humor. As a consequence, Alice's strong-willed nature began to mellow; she experienced a second youth and became an excellent mother for the four More children.

In the postscript to his epitaph at Chelsea, More praised his two wives and said that it would have been wonderful if the three could have lived together:

> Here lies my beloved wife Jane. I, Thomas More, desire that this tomb should receive me and Alice as well. The first of the two ladies, my wife in the days of my youth,

---

14. Vázquez de Prada, 124.

made me the father of a son and three daughters; the other loved her stepchildren, something unusual in a step-mother, with an intensity rare even in a mother for her own children. The one ended her life by my side, the other continues to share it with me, and in such a way that I am not able to judge whether I loved the first one more or love the second more. How happy the three of us would have been together had destiny and morality allowed it! I pray, therefore, that the grave, like heaven, will reunite us. Death will thus afford us what life could not.

This text shows that More loved both of his wives very much, albeit differently for each, according to their age, character, and status. He loved them as they needed to be loved. From the text one can also deduce that each marriage represented different stages in his own growth in the marriage vocation: The words of a young person "because I love you, you are my wife," in the mature man are transformed into: "I love you because you are my wife." This is the only way that a marriage can grow. It seems that More followed precisely that path. "In his two marriages, to Jane Colt and Alice Middleton, More experienced the growth and maturation that normally occurs in just one."[15]

---

15. Berglar, 110.

Chapter 7

QUEEN VICTORIA AND PRINCE ALBERT (1838)

A woman puts marriage ahead of power

Victoria was born in Kensington Palace, London, on May 24, 1819. She was the only daughter of Prince Edward—the Duke of Kent, fourth son of King George III—and Victoria of Saxony-Coburg-Saalfeld. This duchess came from one of the oldest royal families of Europe, and thus her daughter was related to the royal families of six countries. She had German blood, through both her father and her mother, and she was the niece of Tsar Alexander.

The child was baptized as Alexandrina Victoria in the palace's Hall of the Cupola on June 24, 1819, by the Archbishop of Canterbury. Her family called her Drina. She was fifth in the line of succession to the British crown, but through different events, by the age of three she was already very close to the throne.

When she was eight months old, she lost her father, who died of pneumonia on January 23, 1820. Six months later, her grandfather George III, who by that time was blind and mentally incompetent, passed away. Victoria became the heiress to the throne at the age of ten since neither of her uncles, George IV and William IV, had children.

In her early years Victoria spoke only German, the language of her mother and her governess, Baroness Lehzen. But from the moment her accession to the throne became a great possibility, she began to learn English and other languages.

The vacuum caused by her father's death was amply filled by the energetic character of her mother, aided by her governess:

> The princess gave her mother her dutiful regards; but Lehzen had her heart. The voluble, shrewd daughter of the pastor in Hanover, lavishing her devotion on her royal charge, had reaped her reward in an unbounded confidence and a passionate adoration. The girl would have gone through fire for her "*precious* Lehzen," the "best and truest friend," she declared, that she had had since her birth.[1]

Her mother wished to form her as a Christian queen, developing in her certain virtues and preserving her from the pernicious influence of her uncles and the dissolute environment of the court. The educational regime imposed on Victoria, inspired by a severe Anglicanism, was very strict. Her mother became excessively vigilant and overprotective, which isolated her daughter and reduced her life to the family environment.

As a child Victoria could not take a step in the palace without being accompanied by nannies or her mother. She continued sleeping in her mother's bedroom, and her mother held her hand when going up and down the stairs as her proclamation as queen approached. That dependence

---

1. Lytton Strachey, *Queen Victoria* (New York: Harcourt, Brace & World, 1921), 46.

ended up harming the relationship between mother and daughter, causing a distance between them that increased with the passage of years.

In spite of her mother's overprotectiveness, Victoria demonstrated a strong personality and a zeal for independence—possibly inherited from her mother—which led her to not allow herself to be dominated. In addition she was very intelligent, which increased her self-confidence. At the age of twelve, when she was informed that she was destined to inherit the throne, with great calm she commented: "I will be a good queen." She already demonstrated a presence of mind and a determination that she maintained throughout her life and would be key in her successful work of governing.

As the law did not contemplate the ascension to the throne of an infant, the Law of Regency was promulgated in 1831, which established that the Duchess of Kent, Victoria's mother, would be the Regent of the kingdom during the time Victoria was still a minor. Victoria would have to confront her mother and Conroy, the counselor who tried to force her to sign a regency in favor of her mother that would last until Victoria reached the age of twenty-five, thus keeping her separate from the Court. She only trusted Baroness Lehzen, her tutor. She knew how to fight for her freedom—as a person, a woman, and the heir to the throne—in the midst of harsh conditions and strong pressure linked to political and family interests.

Victoria Meets Her Future Husband and Becomes Queen of England

In 1835, at the age of sixteen, Victoria met her cousin and future spouse, Prince Albert of Saxony-Coburg-Gotha, the nephew of King Leopold of Belgium. What initially seemed to be a union of convenience for political interests became an authentic love story on both sides, with a courtship characterized by frequent conversations and correspondence. The courtship resulted in marriage, followed by a very happy married life.

George IV and William IV, Victoria's uncles, occupied the throne between 1820 and 1837. The latter died on June 20, 1837. Since Princess Victoria had already completed her eighteenth year, a regency was not needed. That same day the Archbishop of Canterbury officially proclaimed Victoria Queen of England. She was crowned on June 28, 1838, in Westminster Abbey. The girl recorded the event in her diary:

> Since it has pleased Providence to place me in this station, I shall do my utmost to fulfil my duty towards my country; I am very young, and perhaps in many, though not in all things, inexperienced, but I am sure that very few have more real good will and more real desire to do what is fit and right than I have.[2]

The Young Queen Astonishes Her Advisers

It was expected that Victoria would correct the decadence of the monarchy in England that had developed in the last three reigns due to the incompetence of the sovereigns. Much was expected of a woman who was not well known:

> The new queen was almost entirely unknown to her subjects. In her public appearances her mother had invariably dominated the scene. Her private life had been that of a novice in a convent; hardly a human being from the

---

2. Strachey, 68–69.

outside world had ever spoken with her. . . . When she suddenly emerged from this deep obscurity, the impression she created was immediate and profound. Her bearing at her first Council filled the whole gathering with astonishment and admiration . . . all were completely carried away. . . . What above all struck everybody with overwhelming force was the contrast between Queen Victoria and her uncles. The nasty old men, debauched and selfish, pigheaded and ridiculous, with their perpetual burden of debts, confusions, and disreputabilities—they had vanished like the snows of winter, and here at last, crowned and radiant, was the spring.[3]

Victoria Becomes an Independent Woman

The new queen put all her trust in Lord Melbourne and Baroness Lehzen, while cutting drastically her dependence on her mother.

When, after her first Council, she crossed the ante-room and found her mother waiting for her, she said:

— And now, Mamma, am I really and truly Queen?

— You see, my dear daughter, that it is so.

— Then, dear Mamma, I hope you will grant me the first request I make to you, as Queen: Let me be by myself for an hour.

Then she reappeared, and gave a significant order: her bed was to be moved out of her mother's room. It was the doom of the Duchess of Kent. The long years of waiting were over at last; the moment of a lifetime had come; her

---

3. Strachey, 71–72.

daughter was Queen of England; and that very moment brought her own annihilation. She found herself, absolutely and irretrievably, shut off from every vestige of influence, of confidence, of power.[4]

Neither complaints nor maneuvers were of use to the Duchess of Kent; her authoritarianism had ended. And when the royal home moved from Kensington to Buckingham Palace a month after the coronation, the duchess was assigned a set of rooms separate from those of the queen. That decision of Victoria's was followed by another no less courageous: She would no longer receive Sir John Conroy. Those changes reinforced Baroness Lehzen's influence over the queen. It was quite significant that Lehzen's bedroom was right next to Victoria's.

At the beginning of the new reign, the government was controlled by the liberal Whig party, which had been exercising power since 1830. The prime minister was William Lamb, Vice-Count of Melbourne, an intelligent, effective, and affable man. These qualities impressed the new queen to the point of leaving matters of state in Lamb's hands: "[Lord Melbourne] became in the twinkling of an eye, the intimate adviser and the daily companion of a young girl who had stepped all at once from a nursery to a throne."[5]

The prime minister exercised a great influence over the politically inexperienced sovereign, who asked for his advice and help in everything. That explains why she chose the company of ladies who shared the "Whig" ideology in those first years, distancing herself from matters of government and appearing unconcerned about daily political life.

---

4. Strachey, 78–79.
5. Strachey, 88–89.

The power of Lord Melbourne soon ended, however. First he had shown himself incapable of controlling the British colonies, and afterward he saw his party lose its majority in Parliament. For these reasons he was dismissed in 1839.

At that time the "Tories" (conservatives) prepared to form a government. The queen commissioned Tory Robert Peel with the task of heading the new cabinet but quickly changed her mind, staunchly refusing to accept Lord Melbourne's resignation. This was the first political crisis of her reign.

To what was her change of mind due? One motive was the so-called "Crisis of the Ladies of the Chamber": Robert Peel had demanded that the "Whig" ladies be replaced by "Tory" ladies, which the queen opposed. Another motive was Peel's manners, which Victoria considered detestable. The queen thus brought to light her temperament and stubbornness, hidden until then, becoming personally involved for the first time in the politics of the country. The situation was resolved through a series of negotiations and agreements that restored Lord Melbourne as prime minister.

Victoria and Albert's Wedding

Albert traveled to London to assist at Victoria's coronation. Three years later, the queen made the decision to marry him. After setting the date for the wedding, Victoria underwent a personal crisis.

> Meanwhile Victoria, in growing agitation, was a prey to temper and to nerves. She grew feverish, and at last Sir James Clark pronounced that she was going to have the measles. But . . . Sir James was wrong in his diagnosis. . . . She was suddenly prostrated by alarm, regret,

and doubt. For two years she had been her own mistress—the two happiest years, by far, of her life. And now it was all to end! . . . She would have to promise that she would honour and obey . . . someone who might, after all, thwart her, oppose her—and how dreadful that would be! Why had she embarked on this hazardous experiment? Why had she not been contented with Lord M.? No doubt, she loved Albert; but she loved power too. At any rate, one thing was certain: she might be Albert's wife, but she would always be Queen of England. He reappeared, in an exquisite uniform, and her hesitations melted in his presence like mist before the sun.[6]

On February 10, 1840, in the Royal Chapel of the palace of St. James in London, the queen married Albert of Saxony. Four days prior to this, she had granted her future husband the title of "His Royal Highness." He would be known as the Prince Consort, although he did not formally receive that title until 1857.

Albert was one of the few men whom Victoria had dealt with in her youth, and the first with whom she had the occasion to speak with alone. The wedding was one more manifestation of her decisive character, since she had to confront the opposition of the English people to her marrying a foreigner.

Victoria was very much in love. She was one of the few queens of her era who married for love. She felt veneration for a man who, besides his good looks, had many good personal qualities; he was very refined and possessed a fine political intelligence. Throughout the entire marriage he was a faithful and exemplary husband.

---

6. Strachey, 151–152.

A Difficult Initial Adaptation to Married Life

Albert initially had to confront unexpected difficulties in his married life. As prince consort he had no specific functions, and the queen continued to leave all matters of state in the hands of Lord Melbourne. She thought Albert's collaboration in the government was unnecessary; in addition she took into account the fact that the English did not like foreigners intervening in their politics. Victoria was content with Albert becoming what she expected: a good husband. But he considered himself undervalued: "Victoria idolized him; but it was understanding that he craved for, not idolatry; and how much did Victoria, filled to the brim though she was with him, understand him?"[7]

In spite of the fact that Albert was bored by the politics of the palace, being left out was very disagreeable to him:

> But it was not only in politics that the Prince discovered that the part cut out for him was a negligible one. Even as husband, he found, his functions were to be of an extremely limited kind. Over the whole of Victoria's private life the Baroness reigned supreme. . . . Since the accession, her power had greatly increased. . . . Albert very soon perceived that he was not master in his own house. Every detail of his own and his wife's existence was supervised by a third person: nothing could be done until the consent of Lehzen had first been obtained. And Victoria, who adored Lehzen with unabated intensity, saw nothing in all this that was wrong.
>
> Nor was the Prince happier in his social surroundings. [He was] a shy foreigner, awkward in ladies' company, unexpansive and self-opinionated. . . .[8]

---

7. Strachey, 178.
8. Strachey, 153–154.

Victoria hid many details of her life from Albert. In addition the couple had very different habits. Albert was a morning person and went to bed early, while Victoria got up late because she was active late into the night. He liked to spend time with scientists and humanists; Victoria preferred the interchange of banalities with those who were always around. London enchanted her; he wanted to reside in Windsor. Therefore it was no surprise that friction and quarrels surfaced between them with a certain frequency. These never caused a marriage crisis, though, because of the great love they had for each other:

> Victoria fought in a condition of inferiority because she was no longer mistress of herself: she was dominated by a very intense emotion which made use of her for its own ends. She was madly in love. . . . An anecdote has come down to us which sums up a fundamental aspect of their relationship: When, in wrath, the Prince one day locked himself into his room, Victoria, no less furious, knocked on the door to be admitted. "Who is there?" he asked. "The Queen of England" was the answer. He did not move, and again there was a hail of knocks. The question and the answer were repeated many times; but at last there was a pause, and then a gentler knocking. "Who is there?" came once more the relentless question. But this time the reply was different. "Your wife, Albert." And the door was immediately opened.[9]

Victoria Has a Change of Heart

Albert began to overcome his political ineptitude when he changed his attitude. He began to study politics and receive

---

9. Strachey, 161.

instruction on the English legal system. For her part, the queen, after discovering valuable new qualities in him, had him attend some of the meetings with the prime ministers; she also asked him to communicate their opinions to the government. Soon he became her political counselor, to the detriment of Lord Melbourne. She realized that she had found the perfect companion, not only in family life but also in politics. "She was no longer Lord M's pupil: she was Albert's wife."[10]

Later on Prince Albert was designated regent in case of the queen's death. Added to Albert's political ability was the queen's respect for the parliamentary mechanism. The couple's mutual decisions created a model of conduct that restored the prestige of the English monarchy. The result was that Peel's return to power in 1841 no longer meant any kind of trauma for Victoria.

The birth of the Prince of Wales in 1841, the couple's first boy, took care of the problem of succession. Edward VII succeeded Victoria in 1901.

In 1842 an important change took place: the queen accepted without conflict a change in the role of Baroness Lehzen. This change was highly beneficial to Victoria and Albert's marriage.

Albert and Victoria loved each other very much during their married life and were able to overcome together a very difficult era in the history of England. They produced four sons and five daughters. Among the personal successes of the prince consort were notably the reform of the organization of the royal household and the organization of the first World Fair, known as the Great Exposition of 1851. Inaugurated by Queen Victoria, she was so enthused that on that day she wrote to her uncle the following:

---

10. Strachey, 195.

The first of May, she said, was "the *greatest* day in our history, the most *beautiful* and *imposing* and *touching* spectacle ever seen, and the triumph of my beloved Albert. . . . It was the *happiest, proudest* day in my life, and I can think of nothing else. Albert's dearest name is immortalized with this *great* conception, *his* own, and my *own* dear country *showed* she was *worthy* of it. The triumph is *immense*."[11]

The Exposition produced great economic benefits, and the inventions presented there served as the basis of the South Kensington Museum.

A Grieving Victoria

In March 1861 Victoria's mother, the Duchess of Kent, died. And on December 14 of that same year, forty-two-year-old Albert died of what was diagnosed as typhoid fever. Victoria was at the bedside of her sick husband until the end.

The loss of her beloved spouse, friend, and advisor affected Victoria immensely. It was the saddest event of her life. From that moment on she always dressed in mourning in memory of her husband and was always accompanied by his photograph. She avoided public appearances, ordered her servants to prepare clean clothes for Albert every day, and went to live outside London in Windsor Palace.

In spite of the sorrow that afflicted her, Victoria reacted with great fortitude and did not let herself be crushed. Her soul of iron remained intact. She thought the best way of rendering homage to the spouse who was gone was to make her own the ideal which had animated him: to work untiringly at the service of her country. She proposed to continue

---

11. Strachey, 148–149.

Albert's work and engrave in everyone's mind his merits and virtues, since in life he had not had that recognition. One of her initiatives was to commission Theodore Martin to write a complete biography, and he worked on it without interruption for fourteen years.

The Widowhood and Final Years of Queen Victoria

The queen personally supervised the internal politics, directed successively by Palmerton, Disraeli, and Gladstone. England progressed in the establishment of economic and political liberalism, favoring a broad political participation and stability of institutions.

The problem of Irish nationalism was handled with success, giving that country a greater autonomy: They confronted the demands of the workers, which arose out of the process of industrialization, by legalizing the first modern unions. They attained the greatest economic development known in the history of the country. They produced a great expansion of the British Empire, which included the coronation of Victoria as Empress of India and the creation of the Commonwealth of Australia. The United Kingdom became the greatest power of its era.

Victoria's reign was one of historic influence and splendor, in which, under a Christian morality, great scientific and technical advances were made. To this was united progress in letters and the arts, with personages such as Kipling, Wilde, and Faraday.

Victoria, endowed with an extraordinary majesty, was a living myth and an authority in world politics, without ceasing to be at the same time a maternal figure. At the age of twelve, she had said she was going to be a good queen, and she fulfilled this promise.

With all the zeal of a convert, Victoria upheld now the standard of moral purity with an inflexibility surpassing, if that were possible, Albert's own. . . . She was more—the embodiment, the living apex of a new era in the generations of mankind. The last vestige of the eighteenth century had disappeared; cynicism and subtlety were shriveled into powder; and duty, industry, morality, and domesticity triumphed over them. The Victorian Age was in full swing.[12]

The long duration of her reign provided England with the stability it had not had for a long time. Queen Victoria spent her last Christmas in Osborne House, the residence that had been designed by Prince Albert on the Isle of Wight. There she died, on January 22, 1901, at the age of eighty-one, with her grandson, Kaiser Wilhelm II of Germany, present at her deathbed, along with her son and successor, King Edward VII. She was buried in the Mausoleum of Frogmore, near Windsor beside her husband.

▪ ▪ ▪

Love Is More Than Political Expediency

The woman who was to be the chief figure of one of the most important reigns of European history did not opt for a marriage of expediency. She wanted to marry as ordinary citizens and the poor do: for love. And she did this in spite of the expectations of the English people, who did not want a foreign prince. Her romance with Prince Albert began with a courtship that included lots of personal contact, despite the isolation to which Victoria's mother subjected her. Their frequent conversations and many letters served to help them

---

12. Strachey, 194–195.

get to know each other better and look forward by common agreement toward their future life as a couple.

Victoria married after two years of her reign. Although she was very much in love, it was difficult to take this step; she was accustomed to giving orders and to living a very independent life, and it cost her "to submit herself"—to give herself with committed love and total self-giving and to share her life with a husband. She, who had so much power, would have to learn to live for another person without using that power, and make sure above all that her spouse was happy. She soon learned that, although committed love brought with it renunciations and sacrifices, it did not result in any kind of slavery.

Spouses oblige themselves freely and voluntarily to love faithfully and forever. The commitment is an inexhaustible source of personal growth, while its absence prevents the maturing of love and freedom and makes happiness unattainable. Victoria's initial resistance to replace independence with a shared life was a sign of immaturity about what conjugal life demands, which is not strange since she was so young. Those who marry do not mature as married people by themselves, but in a joint way by living all that marriage entails. Basic decisions have to be shared. Each spouse owes a debt of love to the other.

In spite of her initial reserve regarding married life, Victoria was convinced and excited about her marriage to Albert. This fact shows the great influence admiration has in the process of love. Remember that the queen felt veneration for a man who, aside from a good appearance, had many good qualities. Love was stronger than calculation, although initially not completely, since Victoria was not ready to share the government with her husband. But she soon realized that this attitude was an obstacle to their spousal relationship.

Mutually Learning to Adapt

Victoria loved him, but did she love him as he needed to be loved? Albert hoped in vain that his wife would allow him to share in some political decisions, and because she didn't at first, he felt misunderstood. Love includes understanding, knowing how to put oneself in the place of the person loved in order to harmonize with his or her sentiments. The conjugal relationship improved as soon as Victoria began to seek the opinion and advice of Albert in some questions of government.

He expected Victoria to act not as his queen but as his wife. Recall the incident of her getting him to open his door: All it took was for her to say that she was his wife to get a positive response. The courage and dignity Albert showed in maintaining their dispute on the terrain of their marriage relationship was praiseworthy, but so was the humility and tenderness with which Victoria corrected herself.

These were not the only mistakes Victoria made as a wife. Perhaps the greatest was to place too much importance on her friendship with Baroness Lehzen to the detriment of her relationship with Albert. For instance, on the advice of Lehzen, Victoria hid many things from Albert, thus negatively impacting their communication and confidence.

Victoria Rediscovers Her Husband and Renews Her Love

It is difficult to understand how a woman who was so intelligent and so much in love with her husband permitted a friend to interfere so much in her private life. Eventually Victoria corrected that error when, in 1842, she accepted the removal of Baroness Lehzen from the position she was occupying. Only then, in view of the improvement produced in her married life, did the queen become conscious of the seriousness of the error she had committed:

> The early discords had passed away completely—resolved into the absolute harmony of married life. Victoria, overcome by a new, unimagined revelation, had surrendered her whole soul to her husband. The beauty and charm which so suddenly had made her his at first were, she now saw, no more than but the outward manifestation of the true Albert. There was an inward beauty, an inward glory which, blind that she was, she had then but dimly apprehended, but of which now she was aware in every fibre of her being—he was good, he was great! How could she ever have dreamt of setting up her will against his wisdom, her ignorance against his knowledge, her fancies against his perfect taste? . . . She who now was only happy in the country, she who jumped out of bed every morning . . . to take a walk, before breakfast, with Albert alone! How wonderful it was to be taught by him! To be told by him which trees were which, and to learn all about the bees! And then to sit doing cross-stitch while he read aloud to her Hallam's Constitutional History of England![13]

Victoria confessed that, in spite of being very much in love, she had some years of blindness regarding Albert. Such "blind love" is more proper to the phase of initial falling in love—the courtship—than to marriage, but in this case it was not so. Victoria's friend was the blindfold that prevented her from getting to know her husband deeply. When that blindfold was removed, she discovered that the object of her love had been more the exterior attractiveness than the interior. That late discovery led to a second falling in love—a revitalization of the previous love.

---

13. Strachey, 169.

Victoria and Albert's story makes it clear that, in marriage, it is not enough just to be in love; one has to accept with humility that human love is always imperfect and therefore improvable. A happy marriage is not one that hasn't experienced any mistakes, but one that recognizes and corrects them again and again.

A Sorrowful Widowed Queen

The marriage union is the strongest human bond that exists. Those who are married are united—they are two natures in one flesh. Therefore the death of one spouse is felt by the other as a tearing apart of his or her very self. This feeling is greater when the spouses have been very much in love and the marriage has been lasting and happy. For the surviving spouse, the death of the beloved is a tragedy that can cause the sorrowing spouse to question the meaning of his or her own life. This was the great sorrow experienced by Victoria at the death of Albert:

> The death of the Prince Consort was the central turning point in the history of Queen Victoria. She herself felt that her true life had ceased with that of her husband's, and that the remainder of her days upon earth was of a twilight nature—an epilogue to a drama that was done.[14]

Victoria always missed the help and especially the love of her lost husband. Her permanent mourning brought much criticism that she rejected.

> Would the world never understand? It was not mere sorrow that kept her so strangely sequestered; it was devotion, it was self-immolation; it was the laborious legacy of love.[15]

---

14. Strachey, 297
15. Strachey, 313.

Chapter 8

---- ❦ ----

NICHOLAS II OF RUSSIA AND
ALEXANDRA FEODOROVNA (1894)

A beautiful and tragic story of love

Nicholas II was born on May 6, 1868, in the imperial palace of Tsarskoye Selo. He was the first son of
Alexander III and Dammar of Denmark—a name she
changed to Maria Feodorovna shortly before marrying. After
the birth of Nicholas, the couple had five more children.

Nicholas was educated in the rigid manners of the Russian Court but isolated from the agitated internal situation
of the Empire. He studied languages, geography, history, and
mathematics. He learned to speak English, French, and German well and acquired a great cultural sensibility. His trips
to England, Japan, and India, carried out from the time of
his adolescence, were of great help in this regard.

He showed himself to be a good student from the beginning. He learned the history of his people and was impressed
by the stories of heroism. In March 1881, at the age of thirteen, he had a terrible experience which marked him for
life: he saw his grandfather Alexander II's assasination by
terrorists. It's possible that this tragic event contributed to
forming Nicholas's fatalistic mentality.

His tutor, Constantine Pobedonostsev, was a philosopher and procurator of the Holy Synod. He instructed Nicholas in the autocratic convictions of the Romanov dynasty and the doctrine of the divine origin of the tsar's power. He taught him that since God chose the tsar, there was no place for representatives of the people to participate in the governing of the nation. If a tsar did not behave as an autocrat, he would not fulfill his duties toward God.

Nicholas's father, Alexander III, was a corpulent, strong man of great character, decisive and with a great capacity for work. He showed himself to be a good father. His mother, Maria, was small, intelligent, affectionate, and cheerful. The family lived in the palace of Gatchina. Although the building contained 900 rooms, they only occupied the mezzanine, previously meant for the servants.

The children were educated in a Spartan way by their father, thus acquiring the virtues of sobriety and simplicity. They bathed with cold water and slept on cots with hard mattresses. Maria took care of them, helped them in their studies, and received their confidences. Her gentle treatment compensated for the severe conduct of her husband. Nicholas possessed a dreamy and artistic character; he inherited his father's mystical authoritarianism but not his capacity to command as a ruler.

In 1882 Maria Feodorovna presented Nicholas with a very beautiful journal. The boy thanked her for it and noted that it would be his diary. The annotations of his diaries became historical documents of great value.

Love at First Sight

Two years later Nicholas went to St. Petersburg to attend the wedding of his paternal uncle Sergei Alexandrovich

Romanov and the German princess Elizabeth. There he met the bride's younger sister, Alix, who was twelve years old. She was the daughter of Grand Duke Louis IV of Hesse and Princess Alice of England. Alix told Nicholas that she was born in Germany on July 6, 1872, and had been baptized Alix, a German variant of Alice. Her mother had died at the age of thirty-five from diphtheria when Alix was only six years old. From that moment on, her grandmother, Queen Victoria of England, took charge of her custody and education, and Alix became her favorite granddaughter.

For Nicholas and Alix it was love at first sight. They met again a few days later in a country house. Five years went by without them seeing each other, but they did not forget each other. During this period Nicholas did his military service in the St. Petersburg Guard. At the age of nineteen, his father conferred on him the rank of colonel and gave him command of a squadron of the Horse Guards.

On October 17, 1888, Nicholas and his family were miraculously saved from an accident. The imperial train in which they were traveling was derailed in Kharkov. The roof of their car went underwater, but Tsar Alexander III, making use of his great physical strength, raised it on his shoulders and held it up until his wife and children were able to escape. That great effort seriously affected his health.

In 1889, at the age of twenty-one, Nicholas was still in love with Alix. She had rejected several proposals of marriage planned by Queen Victoria with other royal houses. By this she showed she had character. Her timidity made her appear cold and distant, but this did not correspond with reality.

When she was seventeen, Alix went to see Nicholas at Peterhof in the company of the imperial family. The initiative for this meeting came from Grand Duchess Elizabeth. During the six weeks they were together, they reaffirmed their love. A solid romantic relationship had developed between them. From this moment on, Nicholas made frequent visits to the home of his Aunt Elizabeth and Uncle Sergei to see Alix. In 1892 Nicholas made this annotation in his diary: "I dream of marrying Alix of H."

Opposition from the Tsar

The young lovers met with opposition from the tsar and tsarina, who had other marriage plans for their son. They were not pleased with a German princess who, in addition, had received a liberal English education. Since they desired an alliance between Russia and France, they had planned to offer Nicholas Princess Helena of Orleans, the daughter of the pretender to the crown of France, the Count of Paris. She was the most suitable spouse to attain their political plans.

The tsar based his opposition to Nicholas and Alexandra's marriage on the fact that the religious difference of the two was an impediment to the wedding—the princess belonged to the Anglican Church and Nicholas to the Orthodox Church of Russia.

Alix did not want to renounce her faith, and therefore she returned to England, where she refused to accept any other suitor. Nicholas gave in to his father's desire but opposed marrying the Princess of Orleans. In addition, he did not give up the idea of marrying Alix some day, choosing instead to wait for the most opportune moment.

Hoping to make Nicholas forget Alix, the tsar organized a trip, together with his brother George, through different countries. It was a chance for Nicholas to get acquainted with different cultures. However, at the beginning of 1894

Tsar Alexander unexpectedly found himself gravely ill with
kidney disease. This resulted in the serious problem of
not having the necessary time to prepare his oldest son to
become tsar. In addition, Nicholas did not have the character necessary to be an absolute ruler. In contrast to the
energetic and confident personality of the father, the son
was weak, shy, and insecure.

Ernest M. Halliday, author of *Russia in Revolution*, mentions a dialogue between the sick tsar and the tsarina:

> The Tsar: "We should at least leave our son stably married."
>
> The Tsarina: "But for Nicholas the only woman that he loves
> and considers marrying is Alix . . ."
>
> The Tsar: "Let's accept her."

Nicholas Asks for the Hand of Alix

In the face of Nicholas's continued urging, in November
1894 Alix converted to the Orthodox religion, although
with the condition of not interiorly renouncing her Anglican faith.

Very close to death, the tsar gave Nicholas his paternal
blessing. A few days later, on April 2, 1894, the tsarevich left
for Coburg with the official task of representing his father
at the wedding of the Grand Duke of Hesse, Alix's brother,
but officially he also intended to ask for the hand of Alix
according to law and custom. But it was hard for Nicholas
to declare his love for his chosen wife in such a public way.
It was also difficult for Alix to give a definitive yes because
of the confusion she felt with regard to the religious question. Given the indecision of the couple, Emperor Wilhelm
II decided to take action: He took Nicholas by his arm, led
him to his alcove, had him leave his sword and fur hat there,

and, putting a bouquet of roses in his hand, said: "Now let's go: we're going to ask for Alix's hand."[1]

That evening, April 8, 1894, the engagement was officially announced.

Nicholas Becomes a Tsar and a Husband

On October 20, 1894, Tsar Alexander III died in the palace of Livadia. Grand Duke Alexander Mikhailovitch wrote:

> The death of Alexander definitively fixed the future of Russia. Among the multitude of parents, courtesans, doctors and servants who surrounded the Tsar on his deathbed, everyone, when all is said and done, realized that the nation had lost in his person, the only support that could prevent Russia from falling into the abyss. Niki (Nicholas) himself, realized that more than anyone. On this occasion, for the first time in my life, I saw the tears in his gray eyes. He took me by an arm and led me to his room, we embraced and wept together. He could not put order in his ideas. He understood that he had become the emperor and the terrible weight of responsibility choked him: "Sandro, what should I do?" he lamented pathetically. "What will become of Russia? I am not yet ready to be Tsar. I don't even know how to speak to the ministers."[2]

The day after his father's death, the tsarevich was installed as tsar, adopting the name of Nicholas II. From this moment he began a tragic adventure, not knowing the enormous forces he would have to confront. In spite of the fact that he had a fatalistic belief in his personal destiny—due to the attempts

---

1. M. Essad Bey, *Nicolas II: Vida y Tragedia*, Joaquin Gil, editor (Barcelona: Iberia, 1941), 72.
2. Essad Bey, 80.

against the lives of his predecessors—he could not imagine the role reserved to him by history: the loss of the empire, the end of the Romanov dynasty, and his personal execution along with that of his family at the hands of the revolutionaries who would put an end to the values of old Russia.

Nicholas would be a patriot and a monarch concerned for the welfare of his people, but he lacked the knowledge and the capacity to react creatively to the new realities that were surging through Russian society.

On November 14, 1894, Nicholas married Alix of Hesse who, upon adopting the Russian Orthodox religion, took the name of Alexandra Feodorovna. Thus she became the Tsarina Alexandra.

The newly married couple was received by Empress Maria Feodorovna (who had opposed the marriage) and part of the Russian court. Alix never forgot that humiliation. That resentment, combined with her reserved character, made the new tsarina avoid the ceremonies of court life, which in turn, generated ill feelings among the nobility. Nicholas and Alexandra's first four children were girls: Olga (1895), Tatiana (1897), Maria (1899), and Anastasia (1901). They worried about not having a son to inherit the throne until 1904, when Alexei was born. The succession appeared to be assured.

The First Stage of Nicholas II's Reign

The beginning of Nicholas's reign was tranquil. A process of accelerated industrialization began that brought the country into the modern world, including the appearance of important worker's movements in the form of unions.

But revolutionary groups were taking advantage of the industrial concentrations as well as agrarian reform movements in order to use discontent for their ideological purposes. The revolutionary socialists opposed the completion of the Trans-Siberian railroad that was being built at the time.

The considerable push that Nicholas's government gave to education, doubling the number of students in secondary and higher education, did not slow the political activity of the revolutionaries in the universities.

Nicholas continued the autocratic line of his predecessors. Proposals to establish a constitution with a limited monarchy were rejected by the tsar. His rigidity in this regard led some important sectors of society—that were not revolutionary themselves—to ally themselves with the more extreme groups.

Nicholas spent long hours working at a particular task. Because he considered it divinely inspired, he resisted delegating it to others, and this was one of the errors that helped bring about the end of the empire. He went over the heads of his ministers, believing that this was a way of being closer to his people. He sought a patriarchal union between the tsar and his people.

The tsar concentrated on the bureaucratic work of reading reports and signing laws and thus didn't get to know the real problems of people. When riots occurred he limited himself to sending troops to repress them. These decisions aided the agitators by increasing their recruits.

On February 14, 1901, the first open rebellion against the imperial government occurred with the wounding of a cabinet minister by a student. A month-and-a-half later, a student assassinated another minister. A year later Count Leo Tolstoy wrote Nicholas a letter, in which he pointed out:

> One third of Russia was in what was called a state of "accentuated protection," which means outside of the law.

The prisons, deportation centers and presidios are full, not only of hundreds of thousands of common criminals, but of political prisoners, among whom are now found workers. Today censors suspend everything arbitrarily, something which has not happened in the worst periods of the last forty years. . . . The result of this whole cruel administration is that the farmers, those 100 million people on whom the power of Russia rests, are becoming poorer year after year, hunger is taking over our country as a regular and almost normal phenomenon.[3]

The tsar could not arrest the author of the books that he himself read to the tsarina during family evenings. Instead he ordered that freedom of expression be granted to Tolstoy.

In 1905, concerned about the defense of Russian ports against the Japanese advance in China, Nicholas declared war on Japan, believing he would obtain an easy victory. His poor information led to the defeat of the Russian Pacific Fleet.

Sorrow Enters Nicholas and Alix's Peaceful Family Life

Alix's life, after the premature death of her mother and her sister May in the same year, had been a succession of sorrows. Finally joy arrived with marriage to a man she loved deeply. Between the two of them, they had created a united and happy family.

But a new suffering soon appeared. Two months after his birth, they discovered that the long-awaited male child, destined to inherit the empire, was affected with hemophilia, an infirmity inherited from his grandmother Victoria. The

---

3. Essad Bey, 138–139.

risk of having an unstoppable hemorrhage meant that the boy could not engage in normal activities for his age. The tsar and his family did not let the people know that the heir was sick.

With the aid of doctors, the anguished parents fought for years against the sickness, but no cure was found. One day Alexei suffered a relapse so serious the doctors said the situation was hopeless. That moved the parents to seek the help of a faith healer, Grigori Rasputin. When he arrived the child's pain and convulsions ceased. This was repeated various times, and this led the tsarina especially to believe in Rasputin and consider him someone sent by God.

Bloody Sunday

On Sunday, January 9, 1905, a grave event occurred which may well have been decisive for the Romanov dynasty. A large but peaceful demonstration of peasants and workers, led by an Orthodox priest, walked toward the Winter Palace of the tsar in St. Petersburg to present him with a series of petitions of a non-extremist nature. They carried crosses, icons, and portraits of the tsar and walked in silence, confident that no one would dare to fire upon those portraits. When the crowd was about a hundred yards from the entrance to the palace, they found it being defended by Cossack troops. Without provocation, the soldiers fired on the demonstrators, killing ninety-two of them and wounding several hundred others.

This gave the revolutionary opposition new ammunition against the tsarist regime. It led to a rupture of the previously good relations between the people and the tsar. This was followed by assassinations, including that of Nicholas's uncle, the Grand Duke Sergei Romanov. There were also uprisings of sailors in the ports, among them the cruiser Potemkin, and a major strike which paralyzed industry for a time. These things combined with the costly failed war against Japan showed that Nicholas's regime had not adapted to the economic changes in the country. To try to contain the unrest, Nicholas dismissed the minister of the interior and replaced him with Sergei Witte, a modernizer who advocated the creation of an elected parliament, the Duma. However, the victory of the left-wing parties in the elections for the Duma led to Witte's resignation as chairman of the Council of Ministers.

Witte was replaced by Stolypin, who organized a repressive regime aimed at the revolutionaries. Stolypin promoted a successful agrarian reform aimed at gaining the support of the masses, but he was assassinated in September 1911 in a theater, in front of the tsar.

Entrance into the First World War

The assassination of Archduke Franz Ferdinand of Austria by Serbian nationalists put Nicholas in a difficult situation due to his treaty with the Serbs. On July 31, 1914, the tsar committed the error of mobilizing troops on the Austrian frontier, which led to war with Germany and the beginning of the First World War.

The Russian army gained some victories against Austria in the beginning, but an attempt to advance into Germany led to serious defeats and great loss of life. This brought increased opposition to the tsarist regime. By the beginning of 1917, the government started to disintegrate. The fourth Duma ceded to the pressure of the revolutionaries and formed a provisional government in March 1917 run by Alexander Kerensky, a moderate revolutionary.

Dedicated exclusively to the directing of military operations, Nicholas seemed to lack information about the opposition's movements in the capital. This explains his surprise when the Duma and most of the army's senior staff demanded Nicholas's abdication in order to avoid a civil war.

With the calm and dignity he always exhibited in the most difficult moments, Nicholas II abdicated the throne, for himself and his son Alexei, in favor of his brother, the Grand Duke Michael.

The tsarina remained in the palace of Tsarskoe Selo, isolated and with four sick children. Although she did not know of Nicholas's abdication, she was filled with concern because a segment of the palace garrison had joined the revolutionaries.

It was the Grand Duke Paul who told the tsarina about her husband's abdication. A few days later the tsar appeared unexpectedly at the palace. The soldiers who were guarding the building prohibited him from remaining there. From that moment Nicholas and his family became prisoners, first of the provisional government and later of the Bolshevik government.

Nicholas, together with his family, was first confined in the palace of Tsarskoe Selo, on the outskirts of St. Petersburg. In August 1917, fearing an assassination attempt, Kerensky ordered the imperial family to be exiled in Tobolsk in Siberia. Before leaving he warned Nicholas: "The Soviets want my head; afterward they will come for you and for your family."

Kerensky asked British Prime Minister Lloyd George for asylum for the royal family, but the request was declined. Neither was the same request accepted by the French government.

With the triumph of the second revolution in October when the Bolsheviks, led by Lenin, took over from the Kerensky government, the new Soviet government ordered that the imperial family be moved to the city of Ekaterinenburg, which was under the control of the Red Army. In that way they avoided the risk of the tsar being liberated by counterrevolutionary forces.

On July 4, 1918, a squad commanded by Yakov Yurovski relieved the guard of the house-prison of the imperial family. Then, on the 13th of that month, they received an order from the Soviet of the Urals to execute the whole family. That same day Fr. Skorocev was permitted to celebrate the Orthodox liturgy. At its end the priest offered the tsar the crucifix, Nicholas blessed it and received with the sacred host the blessing of the Russian Church.

On the evening of July 17, with the pretext that a photograph needed to be taken, the family and some of its staff were taken to the basement of the house; without suspecting what awaited them, Nicholas carried Alexei in his arms. They were all shot, together with some servants, a doctor, and the boy's dog—twelve persons in total.

Yurovski first told the tsar that the Russian people had condemned him to death. Following this he shot him at close range with his revolver. Then seventeen soldiers armed with rifles shot the others and bayoneted those who were still alive. (The girls had jewels sewn into their clothing and therefore did not immediately die from the initial shots.)

Their bodies were loaded on trucks and taken to an abandoned mine. On the following day Yurovski ordered the bodies to be burned and destroyed with acid and buried in a secret burial place. Soviet newspapers reported the execution of the tsar, but said that his wife and children had been transported to a safe place.

Discovery of the Bodies

In 1979 two Russian historians found the possible grave of the imperial family in a forest. This was not made public until 1989 when this was published in the newspapers. The grave was opened by Russian authorities in 1991, and nine bodies were found. The missing bodies—of Alexei and his sister Maria—were found in 2007. All of the discoveries were confirmed by DNA samples.

Since 1997 Nicholas and the rest of his family have been buried in the Cathedral of Sts. Peter and Paul in St. Petersburg, where most of the Romanov tsars are buried.

Canonized as Martyrs

In 1981 the Orthodox Church of Russia in exile canonized the members of the Romanov family as martyrs. That decision was endorsed in 2000 by the Synod of the Russian Orthodox Church.

On October 1, 2008, the Supreme Tribunal of Justice of the Russian Federation rehabilitated[4] Nicholas II and his family. This was in answer to a complaint filed in 2005 by Grand Duchess Maria Vladimirovna's lawyer, who considers herself the heir of Nicholas II.

∎ ∎ ∎

---

4. **Political rehabilitation** is the process by which a member of a political organization or government who has fallen into disgrace, is restored to public life. It is usually applied to leaders or other prominent individuals who regain their prominence after a period in which they have no influence or standing. See *http://en.wikipedia.org/wiki/Politicalrehabilitation*.

A Long, Loving Courtship that Ended in a Wedding

From the time they met in 1884 until they married, Nicholas and Alix spent ten long years making a great effort to maintain their relationship and protect it from difficulties and dangers. These included distance, time, the opposition of both of their families (who desired a marriage of convenience), and religious differences.

The year 1894 was especially intense, with important events that put the couple's emotional control and trust in each other to the test. The culmination was their wedding, which was preceded by Alix's conversion to the Orthodox religion, the gravely ill tsar's acceptance of their marriage, Nicholas's request for the hand of Alix, the tsar's death, and Nicholas's accession to the throne.

> Not a shadow, nor a presentiment disturbed the happiness of the two lovers. The slow agony of the Tsar, the difficult days that awaited the two children, the immense country, awaiting in an anxious expectation, all this seemed to belong to another planet. . . . This love was for Nicholas a happy island in which no pain, no bitter chance of fate should disturb their peace. This enchanted retreat of two beings in the midst of the devastating storms of the contemporary era lasted 24 years and constitutes perhaps the strangest phenomenon in the mysterious mental life of the Tsar. The prelude to this idyll began when Nicholas left England to reunite with his family in the Crimea.[5]

The capacity that people who are really in love have to isolate themselves from all that surrounds them and to

---

5. Essad Bey, 75.

concentrate on their relationship, elevating it spiritually above very difficult events, is impressive. It is as if they have been touched by a magic wand that preserves them from the evils that lie in wait for the rest of mortals.

The story of Nicholas and Alexandria's love could not have started more romantically: with a love at first sight at the beginning of adolescence when they were sixteen and twelve years old respectively. The phenomenon of "Cupid's bow" is not always the beginning of a stable and continuous love, since it is based principally on acquaintance and physical attraction; such insufficient knowledge goes into the imagination, idealizing the person loved. What blossoms is an emotional love, while rational and voluntary love is scarcely present.

In many cases, the relationship disappears, either through inconsistency or lack of physical contact. But in other cases it continues to grow and flourish. What contributes to that continuity is personal contact, sustained by frequent conversation. That contact helps each lover to go on discovering in a progressive way the real "I" of the other. After getting to know each other in a more objective way, the couple is in a position to decide whether they accept each other mutually as they are and whether both of them are compatible within a single setting of love.

In Nicholas and Alix's case, the conditions for an eventual outcome of marriage were present. They maintained a prolonged courtship with lots of personal contact and frequent meetings, in spite of the distance. That permitted them to get to know each other better and test whether they really loved each other. Theirs was a love that knew how to wait without weakening and falling into forgetfulness. First there were five years without seeing each other because of Nicholas's military obligations; later there were another five when they resisted together the opposition of the tsar and the tsarina and awaited a solution to the problem of their different religions. The marriage commitment of April 8, 1894, was the happy end of a long, loving struggle that showed the couple's constancy. On the evening of that day, Nicholas made the following annotation in his diary: "An admirable, unforgettable day of my life, that of my engagement with my beloved Alice. All day I have been walking around like a drunk, not able to understand exactly what has happened to me. I can't believe it; I have a fiancée."

Essad Bey comments as follows on this note of the tsarevich:

> With this brief note, by which he expresses his excitement and his joy, there begins the personal happiness of this most ill-fated of all the Tsars. He was faithful to this family happiness. He did not abandon it, neither during the storms of the revolution, nor during the war, nor after his abdication. He was even faithful on the day when, holding his hand in that of Alice, worn out and pale, he went down to the cellar of the Ipatiev palace to place himself before the deadly bullets.[6]

Conjugal Harmony and Happiness

The relationship between Nicholas and Alix was that of an authentic love, both in the years of their romantic courtship and those of their happy marriage. And that was possible in spite of the painful and incurable illness of their son Alexei. How did this difficulty affect their marriage? It strengthened the union between them.

---

6. Essad Bey, 73.

Their conjugal happiness was not obscured by the grave political convulsions at the end of their reign. This was due, above all, to the faithfulness of a wife who continued to be very much in love and never ceased to express her love:

> In the anxious days of the outbreak of the revolutionary rebellions, Alexandra tenderly recalled the period when she fell in love with Nicholas and married him: "It has been thirty-two years since my heart as a young girl was filled with intense love for you."[7]

On learning of her husband's abdication, she limited herself to commenting: "My poor love, he is alone with his pain." Later she informed her children of the change that would take place in their lives.

When Nicholas arrived by surprise at the palace where his family was staying, the following took place.

> The Tsarina ran to meet him like a girl of sixteen madly in love. They embraced passionately. Later he led her to his alcove and spent four hours with her. During this time the Tsar was crushed by the pain caused by the doom hanging over their destiny.[8]

Nicholas and Alix were happy, although with very different outlooks. While the tsar sought justification of his acts in God's will, the tsarina gave him advice based on logical arguments. Nicholas was insecure, mistrustful, and fatalistic; Alix was characterized by reasoning, pride, and bitterness. Contact with the court greatly irritated her. Within her

---

7. Juan G. de Luaces, *Nicolás II, Zar de Rusia* (Barcelona: Ediciones G. P., 1960), 19–20.

8. Essad Bey, 396.

there was always a conflict between Russian mysticism and a European outlook. Although she tried, the Western princess did not succeed in becoming a true Russian.

> In spite of these differences, the life of the imperial couple followed its course of inalterable happiness. . . . The more overwhelmed Nicholas was by the burden of government, the more he longed for those pleasant hours of family life. The beautiful palace of Tsarskoe Selo, where the imperial family spent the major part of the year, was converted into an idyllic island of love, on whose shores the high waves of the agitated Russian Ocean broke without power.[9]

Each accepted the other as they were, with their character, virtues, defects, and customs. In that way their differences were not a cause of marital conflict but rather a complement between two personalities. They learned to live with those differences. And they attained a true family life, in spite of the great responsibilities of government. They knew how to balance family and work. The family was for them a sphere of love, which renewed them daily after the drain they suffered in the social and political sphere.

Throughout each day both Nicholas and Alix stayed aware of the fact that the priority for them was each other. They kept the memory of their love alive when they were not together and eagerly awaited being reunited. In their long married life, there was no habituation or routine, because they looked at their marriage as a permanent prolongation of that initial "arrow" from Cupid's bow.

Nicholas sent his wife a bouquet of flowers every morning. During work hours each continued thinking of the other. Alix showed impatience while waiting for Nicholas's return

---

9. Essad Bey, 108.

when he was away. Their marital happiness was described by an historian of the epoch in this way:

> There was never a word between the two spouses which was not that of friends. They felt themselves constantly encouraged by each other with the most refined attentions, and avoided wounding each other even by a look. From the beginning of their union until its tragic end together, their words and relationships were always those of two recently married young people on their honeymoon. Never did their love become lukewarm for a single instant.[10]

They took care to have a daily time to be alone together, speaking of everything and enjoying each other's company. In the tsar's diary we see that they used to walk through the garden, contemplating together the setting of the sun and speaking of the things of each day.

---

10. Essad Bey, 109.

Chapter 9

PIERRE CURIE AND MARIE SKLODOWSKA DE CURIE (1895)

A shared passion for science helped them to love each other

Marie Sklodowska was born in Warsaw on November 7, 1867. At the time, most of Poland was occupied by Russia, which had imposed its language and customs and tried to keep the Polish people ignorant of their culture. Many patriotic Poles, such as the parents of Maria, resisted this subjection to the tsar.

Marie—familiarly known as "Manya"—was the fifth child of Wladyslaw Sklodowski, a high school physics and mathematics teacher, and Bronislawa Boguska, a teacher, pianist, and singer. Their five children were Zofia (1862), Jozef (1863), Bronislawa (1865), Helena (1866), and a year later, Marie.

The parents were well educated and fostered in their family an environment of interest in knowledge. For Wladyslaw education was very important. He read to his children the classic authors of universal literature and showed them the apparatus he used in his physics classes.

From very early on Marie showed herself to be a brilliant student with an excellent memory and a great capacity for concentration. To this was added a passion for learning, reflected in her love of reading. She especially enjoyed natural history and physics.

She did her first studies in her native city in a private school. There were at that time two plans of study in Poland: the Polish one, carried out secretly, and the official one, with material imposed by the Russians. The situation was stressful both for teachers and students,[1] since they ran the risk of being discovered by the Russians and sent to jail. For Marie it was even more stressful because, being the most diligent student, she was always chosen to recite some passage in Russian when an inspector visited the school.

In 1873, as a political reprisal, the Russian school supervisor discharged Marie's father from his official position of subinspector of a boy's institute. This obliged the family to rent out rooms and give private classes in their home.

In 1876 Zofia, the eldest sister, died from typhus. A year later, at the age of ten, Marie was transferred to a public school where only Russian was spoken. Throughout her secondary studies, following the example of her brother and sisters, she was always first in her class. In addition, she spoke four languages: Polish, Russian, French, and German.

A Girl Marked by Sorrow

On May 9, 1878, Marie's mother died, a victim of tuberculosis. During her years of sickness, she had avoided all close contact with her children to prevent contagion; she never caressed them nor kissed them. To Marie that attitude was incomprehensible and very sad. The two premature deaths,

---

1. See Robert Reid, *Marie Curie* (London: Camair Press, 1984).

occurring in the space of two years, imprinted on Marie a feature of introversion that always remained with her.

In 1884, at the age of fifteen, Marie finished her secondary studies with a gold medal. That same year she suffered her first nervous breakdown, and her father sent her to stay with some relatives in the country for a year, where she could do horseback riding, rowing, and fishing in a lake.

She returned to Warsaw with a great eagerness to continue her education and study science. Her brother Jozef was able to enter the School of Medicine of the University of Warsaw, but she and Bronia could not because they were women. Marie eluded the prohibition of the authorities by studying in secret. She was enrolled in the clandestine "Floating University" of Warsaw. During this period she was interested in positivistic theories.

The two sisters dreamed of studying at the Sorbonne of Paris, although they knew that their parents could not afford it. They conceived a plan to accomplish this, based on mutual help.

The Sacrifice of Working as a Governess

In 1885 Marie took a job as a governess, with the intention of alleviating her family's financial difficulties, but also with the desire of financing Bronia's stay in Paris. The two sisters had reached an agreement: Bronia would study medicine in Paris while Marie aided her from Poland; when Bronia finished her studies, it would be Marie's turn.

Her first job as a governess was disappointing. On December 10, 1885, she wrote about it to her cousin Henrietta in a letter that was included in the biography written by her daughter Eva Curie:

Since we separated, my life has been that of a prisoner. As you know, they placed me in the house of the B's, the family of a lawyer. I would not desire such a hell for my worst enemy. My relations with Mrs. B. have become so cold that, not being able to put up with her, I told her so. . . . I have gained something by getting to know the human species a little better. I have learned that the people described in novels exist, and that one should not enter into contact with people who have been demoralized by fortune.

Eva commented on that episode:

Coming from a person without any bad streak, it shows us the innocence of Manya and her illusions. Placed at random in a well-off Polish family, she thought she would meet sympathetic people, lovely children. She was ready to take an interest in them, to like them. Her deception was a rather hard blow.[2]

After leaving that first job, where she stayed only a few days, she applied for another position as a governess, with much better pay but some eighty miles from Warsaw, out in the country. To accept it meant totally isolating herself from her family. She took a train on January 1, 1886, fearing that her new employers would be like the previous ones. After three hours by train, there followed four hours by sleigh during a winter's night.

The Zorawski family, besides being wealthy, had another set of values that pleased Marie from the first moment. In a letter to her cousin Henry, written on February 3, 1886, Marie said that she lived in Szczuki, that she had gotten used

---

2. Eva Curie, *La Vida Heroica de Maria Curie* (Buenos Aires: Espasa-Calpe, Coleccion Austral, 1944), 57.

to the new work, that the Zorawskis were excellent persons and very well educated, that she was in charge of three girls, and that Mr. Zorawski was an agricultural engineer, who was farming five hundred acres of sugar beets destined to a nearby sugar factory of which he was the majority stockholder.

Continuing, she described what she saw from the house.

> Isn't it funny to come to an isolated country house; imagining in advance a rugged landscape, meadows, and forests, and then, on opening the balcony for the first time, discover a tall, aggressive factory chimney, fouling the sky with its opaque plume of black smoke? For two miles around there is not a mountain, not even a meadow. Nothing but sugar beets and more sugar beets, which cover these large monotonous fields. In the Fall these pale, earthy beets, piled on carts pulled by oxen, slowly converge toward the factory, which is a sugar mill. Near these sad buildings of red brick are grouped the shacks of the village of Krasiniec. And even the river itself is a slave of the factory where it arrives clean and leaves dirty, covered with a cloudy and sticky foam.[3]

During that time Marie took advantage of her free time to write many letters to her family. She also studied physics and mathematics on her own, thanks to the fact that she could borrow books from the factory library. She even had time to set up a small, secret school where she taught Polish to the children and adolescents of the village, most of whom were illiterate. The Zorawskis permitted her to hold that school in their house, knowing that, if reported, they would all be sent to Siberia. But Marie's dream was not to be a professor but a student—at the University of Paris. At

---

3. Curie, 61.

times she lost hope, being forced to study out-of-date manuals without any guidance.

A Loving Deception

Love did not enter into Marie's plans, but it arrived at the beginning of 1887, through a romantic idyll with Casimir, the oldest son of the Zorawskis. He had just returned from Warsaw, after ending his studies of the same scientific materials Marie was passionate about. Casimir was dazzled by the athletic and educated governess, so different from the girls he knew. They were the same age, nineteen, and they soon made plans for marriage. Although Marie was conscious of being in an inferior social position, her concern was lessened by the fact that everyone in that family seemed to like her.

When Casimir asked his parents' approval of their relationship, he received a negative response:

> In an instant, in that house in which they took pride in treating Marie like a friend, impassable social barriers arose. The fact that the girl was of a good family, educated, brilliant and with an unsullied reputation; the fact that her father was widely known in Warsaw as an honorable gentleman, did not count against seven implacable words: It is impossible to marry a governess! Lectured, heckled, shaken, the student saw his resolution sinking. He did not have a strong character. He feared the reproaches and anger of his family. And Manya, wounded by being despised by these people who were inferior to her, closed herself up in a mistaken indifference and a categorical silence. The result was that she never gave thought to this affair again.[4]

---

4. Curie, 68–69.

Casimir's parents ordered him to break his commitment. That very bitter experience of love left a mark on Marie, especially since it was her first love.

Marie wanted to leave Szczuki, but she could not allow herself the luxury of giving up a well-paid job, with which she was financing the studies of her older sister. Therefore she bore the humiliation and stayed in that house as though nothing had happened. It was one of the saddest moments of her life. She had character, but this did not make her invulnerable to feelings.

Eva Curie describes the state of her mother in this way:

> Wounded in love, disappointed in her intellectual dreams, and materially needy since through helping her sister and family she barely had anything left. Manya tried to forget her destiny, this path on which she felt herself stymied forever. Manya turned to her family. She did not ask for help, nor did she even tell of her sorrows. In each of her letters she gives advice freely and offers her help, because she wants her loved ones to have an agreeable life.[5]

In a letter she wrote to her brother Jozef on March 9, 1887, she advised him to remain in Warsaw instead of burying himself in a small town:

> Working in a small village will prevent you from developing your culture and of doing research. You will go downhill in a corner and will not have a career. Without a pharmacy, without a hospital, without books, you will not develop in spite of your strongest resolutions. And if this were to happen, I would suffer enormously, since now I have lost any hope of becoming anything and all my ambition is limited

---

5. Curie, 70.

to your future and Bronia's. It is necessary that you two at least make progress in your lives according to your gifts. It is necessary that those gifts, which undoubtedly exist in our family, never disappear, and that they triumph by way of some of us. The more disappointments there are for me, the more hope I put in you.[6]

A Return to Warsaw and Secret Experiments

In July 1889 Marie's work in Szczuki came to an end, since they no longer needed her services. Thus she returned to Warsaw to continue working and studying on her own.

She began a third job as a governess but gave up that work after a year, since her family's financial situation had improved. Her father accepted a job as head of a correctional institution for boys, with a salary that was large enough to finance Bronia's stay in Paris. Marie limited herself to giving some private classes and was able to renew her relationship with her friends involved in the "Floating University." To this joy another was added: that of being able to carry out simple experiments in physics and chemistry in a small, clandestine laboratory. Years later she confessed that carrying out those first attempts developed her taste for experimental research.

In March 1880 Bronia wrote to Marie from Paris, telling her that she had married a Polish compatriot and inviting her to stay in her house the following year. Marie hesitated and answered that she did not know what to do. She resisted leaving the pleasant environment of Warsaw, close to her family and friends. Finally on December 23, 1881, she wrote

---

6. Curie, 70–71.

Bronia, accepting her hospitality and offering to help her with the housework.

Marie Moves to Paris

A strong vocation in science led Marie to abandon her beloved homeland. In 1891, at the age of twenty-four, she traveled by train to the French capital with her books, some provisions, and a folding chair (since those traveling fourth class were not provided with seats).

Once settled in Paris, she enrolled in the School of Science at the Sorbonne. There she found the intellectual freedom that did not exist in her homeland. She had to take two streetcars to get to her classes. Upon listening to the professors, she discovered there were great deficiencies in her previous preparation and learned she would have to work very hard to obtain a degree in science.

She found that her sister's apartment did not have the quiet needed for study, especially because they had many visitors. In addition it was quite far from the Sorbonne and the transportation costs were high. With her Parisian family's agreement, Marie moved to the Latin Quarter, near the university. Her sister gave her the money necessary for the move.

She found an attic room on the sixth floor of a building, and there she began a life of solitude and poverty, fully concentrating on her studies. She had only forty rubles a month to spend, together with some help from Bronia and her father. She was poor, but no more so than many of the students in her neighborhood. Subsequent rooms she would rent were also very cheap and therefore cold and uncomfortable.

A Life Dedicated to Study and Research

During her first year in Paris, Marie discovered that she could live with very little. Although poorly fed and always cold, she felt motivated and happy with the intellectual challenge she faced, to the point that her nervous problems disappeared.

She dedicated herself to her work with great stubbornness, although it demanded a solitary life without diversions. In the beginning she got together with some Polish students, with whom she spoke of politics, but she began to reduce those gatherings as her interest in scientific subjects increased. By the beginning of her second year, she had cut off all of her friendships in order to avoid distractions. She even gave up cooking and limited herself to eating bread and butter and drinking tea to save time.

But Marie soon began to suffer from anemia. One day, on returning home, she lost consciousness. The previous night she had worked very late and during the day only ate a little bit of vegetables. The doctor who visited her, a friend of her father, accompanied her to the house of Bronia, where she stayed for a week. After recovering, she returned to her attic room to prepare for her exams, promising to be more judicious.

What concerned and occupied Marie at that time? Eva Curie penned these words:

> Working! Working! Entirely sunk in her studies, intoxicated by its progress. Marie felt that she was at a level where she could learn all that mankind had discovered. . . . She felt happy in this atmosphere of secrecy and silence, in this "climate" of the laboratories; until her last day Marie preferred that to everything else. Marie was on her feet, always on her feet, before an oaken table on

which there was a precision instrument, or in front of a Bunsen burner heating some material. Marie was hardly distinguishable under her lab coat of wrinkled fabric from the reflective gentlemen who are bent next to her over other burners and other instruments. Like the rest, Marie respects the recollection of the place. She does not make any noise nor pronounce a single unnecessary word. Not satisfied with one degree, Marie is prepared to pass two: physics and mathematics.[7]

With her great intelligence, sustained by a will of iron, in 1893 Marie accomplished the first great objective that she had proposed to herself: the licentiate in Physical Sciences. In July of that year she returned to her family home in Poland, planning to return to France at the beginning of the school year.

In Warsaw she ran into the problem of how to finance her studies. When she was at the point of renouncing the trip, the miracle occurred: she was granted the Alexandrovich Award for help to meritorious students who wanted to continue their studies abroad. It came with a scholarship of 600 rubles.

On September 15, 1893, she wrote to her brother Jozef. She told him she had rented a room that, compared to the one of the past year, was a palace. She wrote that she was happy to be in Paris and was dedicating many hours to the study of mathematics.

Marie Meets Pierre Curie and Marries Him

At the age of twenty-six, Marie had given up the idea of marriage. After the humiliation received from the Zorawski

---

7. Curie, 98–99.

family, she put love out of her life and let herself be led by her passion for science.

At the beginning of 1894, Marie met Pierre Curie. They were introduced by a Polish professor of physics at the University of Freiburg, Dr. Kowalski, who was spending a few days in Paris. It was a providential meeting. Pierre was thirty-five, nine years older than Marie, and was already a prestigious French scientist, known for his work on crystallography, magnetism, and radioactive materials. He was born in Paris in 1859, the second son of Dr. Eugene Curie, who was passionate about scientific research.

Pierre and his brother Jacques were attracted to the sciences from childhood on. As a result of his experimental work, he had made several inventions. One of them was piezoelectric quartz, which could be used to measure small quantities of electricity with precision. He was also the creator of an ultra-sensitive scientific balance, the "Curie balance." Later the brothers carried out research into magnetism, discovering a fundamental law that came to be known as the "Curie law."

As recognition of fifteen years of successful scientific work, in 1894 Pierre received a salary of 300 francs per month from the French government. When he met Marie, Pierre was still single, because he had not met any woman who shared his passion for science. On one occasion he was said to have remarked: "Women of genius are rare."

The first meeting of the two occurred in Dr. Kowalski's house. Marie relayed it this way:

> When Pierre Curie entered he was on the sill of a door that went out to a balcony. He seemed very young to me, in spite of being 35 years old. I was impressed by the expression of his clear eyes, a slight look of abandonment,

and the fact that he was tall. His speech was a bit slow and reflexive, his simplicity and his smile, at the same time grave and juvenile, inspired confidence. We began a conversation that quickly became friendly. I asked him about certain scientific questions and was enchanted to receive his advice.[8]

The two got along very well from the start. Pierre was agreeably surprised by and attracted to Marie for various reasons: She had come from Poland to study at the Sorbonne, had triumphed in the examinations, and was on the point of obtaining a second licentiate. He was also impressed by her courage and noble spirit. Marie, for her part, admired the deep education of Pierre and his devotion to science. And she felt comfortable with someone with an introverted character such as his.

At Pierre's initiative, friendly meetings between the two followed. Soon he fell in love with her and carried out a persevering courtship. She allowed herself to be loved, but she did not initially accept his proposal of marriage for family reasons. Pierre's ardent and generous love eventually overcame Marie's resistance. They married the same year they met: 1894.

A Good Wife, Homemaker, and Researcher

On returning from their honeymoon in October, they moved into a small, uncomfortable apartment at 24 Galacière Street. They did not decorate the apartment and had only the most necessary furniture. They simplified their daily cleaning routines and were able to dedicate themselves to what interested them the most: scientific research. Their home's principal

---

8. Curie, 107.

decoration was their books. Each day Marie got up very early to go shopping and prepare dinner. She strove to become a good cook with the help of some recipe books.

Little by little Marie became an acceptable homemaker. Later she went to the school's laboratory where she dedicated eight hours to her scientific research. When night came Pierre and Marie prepared their work plan for the following day without ceasing to contemplate each other:

> Often, feeling herself being looked at by the beautiful and profound look of her husband, Marie raised her eyes to receive the message of love and admiration. A silent smile was exchanged between this man and woman who loved each other.[9]

In the second year of their marriage, Marie became pregnant. She was happy about this, but because of illness and fatigue it became difficult to stand in front of the laboratory apparatuses. On September 12, 1897, Marie's daughter Irene was born. She followed in her parents' footsteps, eventually receiving a Nobel Prize in chemistry.

Marie never felt she had to choose between her home and her scientific career. She decided to make them compatible without neglecting either of them. She put passion and will into attaining this objective.

The Doctorate and the Discovery of Radioactivity

In 1898 Marie's chief goal was finishing her doctorate. She asked Pierre, who was the head of her laboratory, for advice on choosing a research project that could serve as the subject of her dissertation. She was very interested in

---

9. Curie, 129.

a recent publication of the French scientist Antoine Henri Becquerel; he detailed his discovery of uranium compounds, including the fact that they emit rays in darkness that could light up a photographic plate. What had to be explained is where that energy came from.

Marie obtained the loan of a small storeroom in the school where Pierre worked to use as a laboratory. Studying uranium rays, she confirmed Becquerel's conclusions but went further. She formulated the hypothesis that the emission of rays from the uranium compounds could be an atomic property of the element, something within the very structure of the atoms. This was a revolutionary hypothesis, given that at the time scientists considered the atom as the most elementary particle and therefore indivisible. No one had imagined the complex structure of atoms and the immense energy within them.

Marie investigated all the known elements to see whether there might be others that emitted rays spontaneously, such as those of uranium. She found that other compounds also emitted them and that that emission seemed to be an atomic property, known as "radioactivity." Pierre, enthused by Marie's project, abandoned his own research projects to help her in the miserable shack without a floor that she had converted into a laboratory.

Most of the experiments had to be carried on outdoors since they did not have any way of expelling harmful gases. The dust and the splashes of acid left marks on their faces, while the vapors attacked their eyes and throat. The two worked in these conditions for four years. In a later letter Marie described the situation:

> We did not have money, a laboratory, nor any assistance to carry out this important and difficult work. It was like

creating something from nothing. . . . I can say without exaggeration that this period was, for my husband and myself, the heroic epoch of our common life. . . . Nevertheless, it was in that miserable and old hangar that we spent the best and happiest years of our lives, entirely dedicated to work. Often we preferred to eat there in order not to interrupt some operation of particular importance. At times I spent a whole day stirring a boiling mass with an iron bar almost as big as I was. By evening I was worn out with fatigue.[10]

Patiently measuring the radioactivity of all of the elements contained in pitchblende, the mineral containing uranium, the Curies discovered two new elements that they named polonium and radium. But they had to prove their existence and determine their atomic weight. In 1902 the Curie couple succeeded in preparing a tenth of a gram of pure radium and were able to determine its atomic weight. From that moment on radium existed officially. The discovery of radium was the result of a tenacious and costly joint effort. It gave birth to a new science that was soon applied to the treatment of malignant tumors.

The two scientists did not wish to patent their discoveries, considering them to be the property of mankind as a whole, especially since they were useful in treating diseases. They thereby renounced great financial benefits. In June 1903 Marie received her doctorate in physics cum laude. The title of her doctoral dissertation was "Research on Radioactive Substances." That subject was the glory of her life. That same year the Curies received the Nobel Prize in physics, shared with Becquerel, for his work with uranium rays. The Curies did not attend the ceremony held

---

10. Curie, 149.

in Stockholm because they were both ill from their intense exposure to radiation. On December 6, 1904, their second daughter, Eva, was born.

The Sudden Death of Pierre Curie and Marie's Life without Him

On April 19, 1906, Pierre Curie was run over by a horse-drawn coach on a Paris street and died. An assistant in the Curie laboratory identified the body, and the dean of the School of Science, Paul Appell, and a friend, Jean Perrin, communicated the news to Marie. Marie, as she had always done, hid her emotions and maintained control of herself. Afterward she asked Jean Perrin to have his wife take care of the little girls that night and leave her alone with her sorrow. An ambulance brought the body of Pierre home for the wake as was customary at that time.

Marie took over Pierre's position as professor at the Sorbonne by unanimous decision of the governing board of the School of Science. She was the first woman to hold a professorship in higher studies. On the day of her first class, the hall was full and there was great expectation about what her first words would be. She surprised her students by saying the same words with which Pierre had ended his last lesson.

The tragic event moved the French government to grant the widow a pension, but she rejected it with these words: "I don't want a pension of any kind. I am sufficiently young to earn my living and support my daughters."[11]

With widowhood Marie Curie's responsibilities increased greatly. She had to sustain her home and continue the research initiated by her husband, but without his help. In

11. Curie, 220.

addition, there awaited her the mission of constructing a laboratory of the level that Pierre had dreamed of, so that the young researchees could carry out their work on the new science of radioactivity:

> With anxiety in her heart and sick of body, she continued alone the work begun, and brilliantly expanded the science created by the couple. The rest of her life was nothing but a perpetual generosity. To the war wounded she offered her devotion and her health. Later she gave her advice, her knowledge and her time to the students, the future scientists who came from all parts of the world.[12]

Pierre's absence caused Marie to have frequent crises of despair and horrible nightmares, but she bore all of this in silence and did not accept sympathy or consolations. In 1910 she published her treaty on radioactivity. A year later she was granted the Nobel Prize in chemistry, becoming the first person to receive it twice. Marie, although unwell, went to Stockholm, accompanied by her sister Bronia and her older daughter, Irene.

The two Nobel Prizes she received aroused the admiration of many people but also the envy and animosity of others. Marie suffered from the prejudices of her epoch: xenophobia and sexism. One of the campaigns against her called her a Russian, a German, a Jew, and a Polack. She was accused of being a foreign usurper during a time when she found herself, weak, alone, and with no defense. In that difficult situation she received the support of her father-in-law, Dr. Eugene Curie, who calmed Marie with his serenity. For Irene and Eva their grandfather was a companion in

---

12. Curie, 9.

play and a teacher during the many hours that their mother was in her laboratory.

With her discoveries Marie sought above all to diminish human suffering. Therefore she promoted the creation in 1914 of an international center for the study of radioactivity, called the Radium Institute, as a part of the University of Paris and the Pasteur Institute. Marie was the director until 1933, and she attended to more than 8,000 sick persons. In 1914, during the First World War, she and her daughter Irene organized a service that offered radiological assistance. They provided x-ray apparatuses to mobile units and hospitals and instructed personnel in their use.

Progressive Blindness Did Not Stop Marie

In 1920 Marie was diagnosed with cataracts in both eyes, which led to a progressive blindness. She only revealed this to her daughters and her sister Bronia. Almost blind and very fatigued she continued going to the laboratory, hiding her limitations as much as she could. In 1921 a group of American women collected a hundred thousand dollars, the value of a gram of radium, and donated it to Marie to fund the Marie Sklodowska Curie Institute of Warsaw. They asked her, in exchange, to visit the United States. Moved by the generosity of these women, Marie made the trip. In 1922 she repeated the same experience. At that time she felt overwhelmed by the appointments, awards, invitations, and acclamations she received. She continued to avoid the glory and sought voluntary isolation in order to be able to do research. In 1933 she transferred the direction of the Radium Institute to her daughter Irene. By this time her health had gotten much worse.

She became blind and died on July 4, 1934, in Sial-anches, France, as a result of radiation-caused anemia. She was buried next to her husband. In 1995 her remains were transferred to the Pantheon of Paris, the first woman to be buried there. It was a final recognition of the researcher who opened the fields of nuclear physics and cancer therapy. A year after her death, her daughter Irene received the Nobel Prize for her discovery of artificial radioactivity.

▪ ▪ ▪

Friendship Leads to Courtship

After the betrayal she suffered in 1887, Marie had dis-carded the idea of marrying. Her move to Paris four years later was motivated exclusively by her vocation to science, not marriage. She was only interested in learning and devoted all of her time to this. Thus when she met Pierre Curie, she saw him only as a companion in her studies and a notable scientist.

Marie's great triumph at the Sorbonne, being a woman, poor, and coming from Poland, made a great impact on Pierre. This showed her great determination and courage. Marie was impressed by Pierre's scientific knowledge. The desire to share their passion for science made them insepa-rable companions. That mutual admiration generated first a deep friendship and only later became love.

In order to continue seeing Marie, Pierre frequently went to the sessions of the Physics Society. A scientific dia-logue and a beautiful friendship developed between them. After obtaining her permission, Pierre went to visit her one day. Her daughter Eva described the romantic scene:

Marie, friendly and discretely, received him in her small apartment, and Pierre, his heart moved on seeing such poverty, nevertheless admired in his heart, the subtle agreement between the person and her environment. In this almost empty area, with her well-worn clothes, her ardent and firm face, Marie appeared more beautiful than ever to him. Her youthful silhouette, wearied by the effort of an ascetic life, could not find a better frame than this bare attic.[13]

Their personal contact increased their intimacy. He influenced Marie's way of thinking; she stimulated Pierre in his work on magnetism. Within a few months Pierre proposed to her. Marie thought marrying a Frenchman would mean abandoning her family and her homeland forever, thus committing treason. Shortly thereafter, without promising him anything, she returned to Warsaw by train, not knowing if she would return to Paris.

Pierre wrote several letters to Marie during that summer. In them there was an insistent request: that she return. On September 7 he wrote:

I advise you to return to Paris in October. It would be very painful to me if you do not return this year. It is not only because of the egoism of a friend that I ask you to come. I just believe that you will work better, and that here you will do more solid and more useful work.[14]

Marie finally decided to return to France. On September 17 Pierre expressed his joy to her:

Your letter from Warsaw, calmed me and I notice that it has also calmed you. I liked your photograph very much.

---

13. Curie, 113.

14. Curie, 117

What an excellent idea of yours to send it to me! I thank you with all my heart. In short, you are coming to Paris and that is a great pleasure for me. I very much wish that we should be, at least, inseparable friends. Do you agree with me?[15]

A Simple Wedding and a Honeymoon by Bicycle

In October 1894 Pierre returned to see Marie at the Sorbonne. He told her he was ready to move to Poland as the price for her accepting his hand in marriage. She was touched by this sacrifice, but she felt that she should not accept it. Ten months later she agreed to their marriage. Marie announced it to her friend Kazia in a letter written in July 1895:

> When you receive this letter, your Manya will have changed her name. I am going to marry the man I spoke to you about last year in Warsaw. It is very painful for me to remain in Paris forever, but what can I do? Destiny has made us deeply attracted to one another and we cannot stand the idea of separating. . . . Write to me at this address: Mme. Curie, School of Physics and Chemistry, rue Lhomond, 42. This is what I will be calling myself from now on. My husband is a professor in this school.[16]

The couple married on July 26, 1895. Marie was happy with the extreme simplicity of their wedding celebration, attended by just a few relatives and friends. The newlyweds took a honeymoon trip on bicycles purchased with the money they received as wedding gifts. This experience predisposed them for the new stage:

---

15. Curie, 118.
16. Curie, 121.

In those happy days there was tied one of the most beautiful knots that ever united a woman and a man. Two hearts beat in unison, two bodies had joined each other, two brains of genius became accustomed to think jointly. Marie could not have married another man who was not this great physicist, this serene and noble being. Pierre could not have united himself with another woman who was not this blonde, gentle, and lively Polish woman, who could be, with some intervals, childish or transcendental, a comrade and a companion, a lover and a teacher.[17]

A Mutual Love

Their shared life never ceased. The loving scene repeated every evening was a very pleasant one: Together they planned their work for the following day, full of admiration for each other. It is a beautiful example of how a couple has to find some time each day to be alone together.

Pierre and Marie understood each other without the need of many words, with a communication that was not very explicit but instead based on hidden shared gestures: an intentional glance, a smile. . . . Each of them knew what that glance and that smile meant. Each of them empathized with the other's feelings and felt solidarity with each other. They experienced a harmony, a communion of souls.

Marie Curie's Sorrowful Loss

The way that Pierre died, the result of an unexpected, brutal, and absurd collision, caused untold suffering for his wife.

---

17. Curie, 125.

The broken body of Pierre made Marie even more conscious of the greatness of his soul:

> Marie had to confront the spectacle of the destroyed body of the man who had caused her to live the years of her life which really mattered. All of the difficulties that they had endured together suddenly seemed insignificant. Pierre had given her the love of his youth and had made her come to a life that perhaps she would never have known in any other way. What remained of that dream was already reaching its end, but what they had lived, they had really shared. . . . The generosity of Pierre had assured the just sharing of an equal task.[18]

When several days had passed, Marie felt the need of expressing the sorrow that was choking her by writing love letters to Pierre in an intimate diary. The pages of the book were stained with tears. Marie would have been incapable of expressing those sentiments if he were alive. She did not write in Polish, her native language, but in French, the language they had always spoken together.

Some fragments were published by Eva in Marie's biography. In one of them, Marie tells Pierre, with great tenderness, how she watched over him at his burial:

> We put you in the shroud on Saturday morning, and I held your head for that transfer. I gave my last kiss to your cold face. Later we put some periwinkles from the garden in the shroud, along with a small picture of myself, the one that you said was that of the "little sensible student" and which you liked so much. It is the photograph that ought to accompany you in the grave, the picture of the one

---

18. Reid, 122–123.

who had the joy of pleasing you so much that you did not hesitate in offering her the sharing of your life when you had only seen her a few times. You told me, very often, that that was the only occasion in your life when you acted without hesitation, with the absolute conviction that you were doing the right thing. My Pierre, I believe that you did not make a mistake. We were made to live together, and our union had to be accomplished.[19]

---

19. Curie, 216–217.

Chapter 10

G.K. CHESTERTON AND FRANCES BLOGG (1901)

They decided to be two in one and succeeded in spite of being very different

Gilbert Keith Chesterton was born on May 29,1874, in Campden Hill, London, into a very conventional middle-class family. He was baptized in the Anglican Church, in spite of the fact that his parents were "freethinkers," in the style of the Victorian era. They did not do this out of religious conviction, but because it was the conventional thing to do, to fulfill a family and social tradition.

Gilbert's father, Edward, had married Marie Louise Grosjean, who was of Swiss-Scottish origin. Edward worked in real estate and had his own agency in Kensington, but his vocation, inherited from his father, Arthur, was art, literature, gardening, and domestic theater.

The Chestertons had three children. The oldest was Beatrice, who died when she was eight years old. Then came Gilbert and Cecil, who never heard Beatrice spoken of because their parents prohibited it. Cecil was Gilbert's intimate friend besides being his brother. They had passionate discussions of cultural matters throughout their adolescence and youth.

Gilbert began his elementary schooling in 1881, and in 1887 he entered St. Paul, a private school, for his secondary studies. He was a solitary student, slow and with poor grades, not well-adapted to the school. In his autobiography he recalls that stage as "being instructed by someone whom I did not know about something that I didn't want to know." He used to sit at the back of the class and distract himself by doing drawings. The teachers considered him a mediocre and backward student. That poor image came also from the slowness of his movements due to his large size—as an adult he reached six foot four and weighed 295 pounds.

Gilbert's talent finally showed itself when he began to give evidence of a prodigious memory and great debating skills. He was one of the founders of the Junior Debating Club and of *The Debater*, the club newspaper, which he began as a joke and ended up having a circulation of a hundred thousand copies. The periodical was of high quality, both in form as well as content—something surprising given that its editors were teenagers. Gilbert also did the illustrations.

A Crisis of Skepticism in an Environment of "Atheist Orthodoxy"

In 1892 Gilbert finished high school and entered college. That meant the dispersion of his group of friends, something that deeply affected Gilbert. Later he confessed that he entered into a period of doubts and temptations, favored by the environment of "atheistic orthodoxy" in which he lived. It was an era of militant agnosticism. The following year he suffered a crisis of skepticism and fell into a deep depression as a consequence of his attraction to spiritualism and the occult. This led him, as he confesses in his autobiography, to "a state of morbid melancholy and idleness, drift and moral anarchy." That same year he began his study of visual arts at the Slade School of Art and began studying English literature.

In 1895 he left the university without having obtained his degree and began working for publishers Redway and T. Fisher Unwin in London and began to publish his works in different newspapers and magazines: *The Speaker, Daily News, Illustrated London News, Eye Witness,* and *New Witness.* He began his journalism career as a critic of visual arts and religious subjects. In spite of the fact that he cultivated almost all the literary genre—biography, the novel, and so on—all his life he was a journalist and an essayist. He wrote short essays with regularity for the newspapers, but the small amount they paid did not allow him to become self-supporting nor to think of marriage.

Love at First Sight

In 1896 Chesterton wrote two poems that expressed his deepest feelings, without any intention of publishing them. One of them was "Suddenly in the Midst" and had the following lines:

> Suddenly I felt lonely.
> Felt like a child in a field with no more games to play
> Because I have not a lady
> to whom to send my thought at that hour
> that she might crown my peace.

The second poem he entitled "Madonna Mia." It included these lines:

About Her whom I have not yet met
I wonder what she is doing
Now, at this sunset hour.

Shortly after this he met the woman he would end up marrying. Her name was Frances Blogg, the daughter of a diamond merchant. Her father had died when she was young, leaving his family in poverty, forcing his three daughters to work in order to live. A friend of Chesterton, Lucien Oldershaw, who was courting Frances's younger sister Ethel, put him in contact with his future bride:

> During the autumn of 1896 Chesterton accompanied Oldershaw to the Blogg family home in Bedford Park, where he met Frances for the first time. He fell in love at first sight. . . . Alone in his room, late at night, Gilbert scribbled his devotion to Frances Blogg.[1]

In the poem that he dedicated to Frances, a young and beautiful practicing Anglican, he explained that God had created the world and put in it kings, peoples, and nations only so that he might thus meet Frances. Shortly thereafter he wrote that "Frances would be the delight of a prince." Gilbert accompanied Frances to church and thus began frequenting the liturgical services.

> From their first meeting, the notebooks of Chesterton are ignited with the subject of love. . . . Both began to live a story that they believed to be unique and unrepeatable. The visits of Chesterton to Bedford Park become more frequent: he began to never miss the Saturday debates and ended by letting himself also come to that "sacred village"

---

1. Joseph Pearce, *Wisdom and Innocence: A Life of G K Chesterton* (San Francisco: Ignatius, 2001), 37.

on Sundays and feast days. The debating club called itself I.D.K. for "I don't know." Frances was very taken by the contrast between his rather disastrous outer aspect and his extremely orderly mind, for it was a true spectacle to see him rebut, one by one and following the same order, the ideas earlier expressed by any participant.[2]

Love gave the young Chesterton confidence in himself and centered his life, especially after his discovery of Jesus of Nazareth.

Commitment and Their Families' Resistance

Between Gilbert Keith Chesterton and Frances a very consistent reciprocal love developed:

> To us two years of romantic growing close and two more years of formal engagement might seem long, but for Gilbert and Frances, that period seemed almost like a summer night's dream, if not to say, in the words of the writer, an eternal instant, or an instantaneous eternity. It was precisely the month of August 1898 that marked the beginning of the count down towards the definitive march together, measuring the time by Springs. It happened in St. James Park, next to a small lake with ducks with a small bridge across it. . . . They had made a date there to lunch together later, as they had been doing from time to time.[3]

Here is an excerpt from the letter he wrote his fiancée a few hours later:

---

2. Luis I. Seco, *Chesterton: Un Escritor para Todos los Tiempos* (Madrid: Palabra, 2005), 88–89.

3. Seco, 91.

I never knew what being happy meant before tonight. Happiness is not at all smug: it is not peaceful or contented, as I have always been till today. Happiness brings not peace but a sword: it shakes you like a rattling dice; it breaks your speech and darkens your sight.[4]

Gilbert was very concerned about obtaining the approval of Frances's family, but as one biographer noted: "Mrs. Blogg poorly digested the sloppiness of that 'stubborn Scarecrow' an objective disaster in presentation, and was terrified at the idea that her daughter might marry him without more revenue than the 25 shillings a week he was then earning in T. Fisher Unwind."[5]

In 1900 Chesterton met Hilaire Belloc, a young French Catholic historian, who helped him to discover Christian social thought and became one of his best friends. On December 24 of that year Gilbert had his first contact with the Catholic Church when he accompanied Belloc to Midnight Mass. On the 25th he told Frances of his decision to marry her as soon as possible.

The Two Become One

Gilbert and Frances were wed in the Kensington parish church on June 28, 1901. He accepted without hesitation the fact that his wife was a practicing Christian. Frances was a wife with many virtues, among them humility and discretion. She is hardly mentioned in her husband's autobiography because she wanted it that way. She wrote many poems but only published a few. She always

---

4. Pearce, 39.
5. Seco, 91.

wanted to remain in the background, where she gave her husband the security he needed and tried to make him happy. Some of Chesterton's verses clearly expressed his idea of marriage:

The world is of the many and of the crazy,
But we are one and we are sane.

As biographer Joseph Pearce noted:

Gilbert and Frances were in a mystical but very real sense One. She exerted on him an influence which was unseen but far greater than that exerted by anyone else in his life. She was the powerful silence in which he found peace.[6]

Frances helped Gilbert come close to Christianity. Because of her he studied the Christian religion with vigor and, later on, she contributed a great deal to his conversion to Catholicism, although he did this four years before she did. She also stimulated her husband's creativity. She inspired him to write beautiful texts about love and marriage. But before this she worked to separate him from Fleet Street, a gathering place for journalists where he became involved in all kinds of excesses. By her initiative, in 1909 they went to live in Beaconsville, twenty-five miles from London, an isolated and peaceful place where Gilbert could live a less crazy life, concentrating on his work and greatly increasing his output. Between 1903 and 1906 Chesterton published biographies of Robert Browning and Charles Dickens as well as his first novel, *The Napoleon of Notting Hill*, about a political character.

6. Pearce, 41, 46.

Chesterton's Defense of Orthodox Christianity

In 1903 Chesterton wrote a polemic against the deterministic thinking of the *Clarion's* founder, Robert Blatchford. Chesterton's arguments show his progression from agnosticism to Christian thought. Since certain skeptics he criticized accused him of judging their view of life without explaining his own, Chesterton did this in his book *Orthodoxy*, published in 1908 and dedicated to his mother. The French philosopher Etienne Gilson considered it the best Christian apologetic work produced in the twentieth century. There Chesterton confesses himself to be a partisan of Christianity without being a Christian; in addition he shows an initial interest in Catholicism, to which he converted in 1922.

In that work Chesterton refutes various anti-Christian theories. One of them connected Christianity with obscurity and sadness. He answered that joy and light are the great secrets of the Christian.

In 1908 one of his best known novels appeared: *The Man Who Was Thursday,* an allegory about evil and free will, which denounced the cultural decadence of the late nineteenth and early twentieth century.

A Nest without Chicks

Another reason for the Chesterton's move to Beaconsfield was Frances's mental and physical health.

> Frances's bouts of depression were nothing new, as she had suffered prolonged periods of anxiety following the tragic deaths of her sister and brother. None the less the cause of the black moods in 1909 was not so obvious. Certainly she

was in a great deal of physical pain, due to the curvature of the spine from which she had long suffered . . . There was, however, one other possible explanation. Frances and Gilbert had always cherished the prospect of starting a family, but their efforts hadn't borne fruit. . . . [Frances] sought solace, and found security, in the creation of a home in Beaconsfield, building a nest even if there were to be no nestlings. From this sound base any remnants of bitterness evaporated and soon other people's children were enlivening the home. In fact, Gilbert and Frances positively welcomed youngsters into their new home, preferring the company of the children to that of their parents.[7]

In 1911 Chesterton published *The Innocence of Father Brown*, bringing together a dozen detective stories featuring a Catholic priest who, while appearing humble and inoffensive, solves the most mysterious crimes thanks to his knowledge of human nature. The detective always encouraged the criminal to rebuild his relationship with God, which showed the value Chesterton placed on forgiveness and confession. Other later stories were collected in *The Wisdom of Father Brown* and *The Scandal of Father Brown*. A number of movies have been made based on these stories.

Between 1913 and 1914 Chesterton collaborated regularly with the *Daily Herald* and began to be known as one of the most polemical journalists in the country. He had the valuable help at this time of Dorothy Collins, an ideal secretary for a disorderly author, whom he came to consider as an adopted daughter. In 1918 during the Second World War his only, and much loved, brother Cecil died.

---

7. Pearce, 112–113.

Chesterton's Conversion to Catholicism

With the passage of years, Chesterton was getting closer and closer to Christianity. He responded to the idea of the superman, proposed by Nietzsche and followed by George Bernard Shaw and H.G. Wells, with the essay "Why Believe in Christianity?" In 1923 he published a biography of St. Francis of Assisi. With that he wanted to show that the life of a saint could be more exciting than the best novel. Ten years later he published a biography of St. Thomas Aquinas, which merited great praise from the eminent Thomistic philosopher Etienne Gilson.

In 1921 he carried on correspondence with three converts to Catholicism who helped to orient his thought toward the faith they professed: Maurice Baring, Fr. John O'Connor and Fr. Ronald Knox. Through O'Connor, Chesterton learned that the Catholic Church has knowledge of both the good and bad by means of the sacrament of penance. Confession had a great attraction for him, since it initiated a new relationship of the believer with his Creator. He was also much influenced by devotion to Mary. He also discovered that Christianity had conquered people's hearts through humility.

In 1922, at the age of forty-six, Chesterton was baptized in a simple building with a corrugated roof, because in Beaconsfield Catholics had not yet been able to build a church. During the previous days he had studied a catechism. In his autobiography he later confessed that a small penny catechism had taught him all that science and pagan philosophy had not. He explained that his conversion from Anglicanism to Roman Catholicism was completely rational and that he did it to get rid of his sins, since no other religious system existed that would make them disappear.

In 1925 he published *The Everlasting Man,* which many consider his masterpiece. In this book he presents a Christian conception of history.

Silver Wedding Anniversary

On June 28, 1926, Gilbert and Frances celebrated their twenty-fifth wedding anniversary. In the autumn of their lives and their marriage, their love continued as vividly as when they were newlyweds, because both of them were committed to this. It is not easy to be the wife of a genius, and Frances knew this when she first met Gilbert in Bedford Park—that very big boy with his shortsighted and kind eyes, so brilliant in debate and so disastrous in everything else, who had fallen in love with her with the impetus of a medieval troubadour. Now as then Chesterton's love continued as strong as ever. He felt so united to Frances that he even postponed conversations until she could join him. To his friend Baring, Gilbert said:

> For more profound reasons than my spirit can explain, I need to attend especially to the thinking of my wife, whose life has in so many ways been a very heroic tragedy, and with whom I have contracted such a debt of honor that I can not support the idea of abandoning her, not even psychologically, and I would like to bring her with me with tact and sympathy.[8]

On November 1, 1926, Frances converted to Catholicism. She was followed by their "adopted daughter," Dorothy. Shortly thereafter, Gilbert and Frances were sacramentally married in the Catholic Church.

In the history of the Chesterton's married life, there were no conflicts, not even during moments of financial problems and sickness. The trials to which life submitted them only served to unite them even more.

---

8. Seco, 295.

Chesterton's Sickness and Death

After writing a hundred books, Chesterton became gravely ill in June 1936. Francis never left his bedside.

> On Saturday, June 13, Chesterton was unconscious. As it got dark, he opened his eyes, looked at Frances and said with a half smile: "Hello, my darling," and then noticing Dorothy, who was there at that moment: "Hello, my dear." Those were his last words. He lost consciousness again, spent the night breathing with great difficulty and, at ten fifteen in the morning [. . .] he passed into the next world. He had just passed his 62nd birthday.[9]

His biographer, Joseph Pearce, gave a positive interpretation to those final words which seemed inadequate:

> There is real bathos in these last words of Chesterton; it is disappointing that one of the greatest wits of the century should make his exit so anticlimactically. Yet the words are sublimely apt, first, because they were addressed solely to the two most important people in his life: his wife and his surrogate daughter, and, second, because they were words of greeting and not of farewell, signifying a beginning and not an end of their relationship. Certainly, all three people in the room believed this to be the case, however hard the reality may have appeared *in extremis*.[10]

Cardinal Arthur Hinsley, Archbishop of Westminster, and Frances received telegrams of condolence from Rome,

---

9. Seco, 360.
10. Pearce, 479.

signed by Cardinal Pacelli, the future Pope Pius XII. A few days after the funeral, Frances wrote to Maisie Ward:

> Each day I find it more difficult to keep going. It is almost unbearable to feel that now he doesn't need me anymore. How do lovers love when they don't have each other? We two were always lovers. I am going to have a Mass offered for him every Tuesday, but I seem to feel that it is more for the repose of my soul than for his.[11]

Chesterton died on June 14, 1936. He had just finished writing his autobiography. In the funeral celebrated in Westminster Cathedral, Ronald Knox read his funeral eulogy and Msgr. O'Connor sang the Requiem. Pope Pius XI granted him the title of *Defensor Fidei*. Frances died two years later, on December 12, cared for by Dorothy. Of her, Fr. O'Connor said: "Gilbert we owe to Frances, because she knew how to foster his genius and to fend off disruptive elements." And Douglas Woodruff said the following: "Frances Chesterton figures among the great wives of our literary history."

▪ ▪ ▪

A Romantic Courtship

Gilbert and Francis showed great intuition and clarity in regard to their falling in love at first sight: Both of them were able to grasp in a very short time what the other had that was singular and valuable. Such intuition and clarity proves that love is not illogical or irrational. The two centered from the first moment not on each other's exterior but on the interior, on their spiritual qualities; what attracted

---

11. Seco, 363.

them led them to love each other. The inevitable idealized love present in all infatuations in this case was transformed, sooner than is usual, into a love based on a real knowledge of the person loved. They knew each other from within, and they accepted each other as they were, with both their virtues and their defects.

Throughout the whole courtship their love tended toward union and was nourished by a deep personal relationship. The courtship was not for them an end in itself, but rather a step preparing them for marriage. The two were courageous and persevering in the face of their families' disapproval.

Gilbert had a marked predisposition to love and to be loved; he demonstrated this by continual personal contact and writing letters. He produced deep reflections on love, which he expressed in poems shared with his loved one; he also adapted himself to Frances's religious practices in spite of being an agnostic. Frances did not let herself be overly influenced by Gilbert's disastrous appearance, his small financial income, or the fact that he was an agnostic. Beyond all that she valued his intelligence, his dialectic capacity, and, above all, his kindness. In this way she showed great character and confidence in her lover. This very positive attitude must have had a great influence in his allowing himself to be infected by her religious beliefs.

A Happy Marriage Between Two Very Different Spouses

Religion was not the only difference between the two.

> She is abstemious by nature, she drinks tea and water and eats just enough to live, without any excess except for

chocolates on special occasions; he, in contrast, likes to try everything, if possible in great quantities and well sprinkled with beer and wine. She is practical, precise and orderly; for him, there are only his thoughts and, despite his good will he messed up everything that he touched. She sees ahead and he, more than for the day, lives for the second, when he is able to come down from the eternity of his cloud. She is punctual and he has no idea of time. She is careful with her clothing and with everything else; he continues to be a disaster and will go in any old way without noticing it. She is of a weak constitution, with rheumatic problems and spinal ills; he defiantly oozes good health and vital force. She relaxes in the fields and flowers; he is one hundred percent urban and, although he loves landscapes, the only flowers that he recognizes are roses, obviously, and one or two others that Frances taught him to identify. . . . In spite of everything, their life together functioned well from the first moment because of the love that they professed and by her well proven knowledge of his limitations.[12]

Both of them, from the time of courtship, learned to accept each other. In that way, they avoided many tensions and conflicts, and their two personalities became complementary. But beyond such positive attitudes stood the quality of their love: a disinterested love that gave itself unconditionally, a love of total self-giving that implied renunciations and self-forgetfulness in order to seek, first of all, the happiness of the other.

How did each spouse contribute to this harmony in the marriage? Frances chose to remain in the background out of love of her husband. From that position she exercised

---

12. Seco, 121–122.

a loving care that brought Gilbert what he most needed: order, security, balance, stimulation of his creative capacity, and help in his spiritual crisis. And she did it while experiencing many hardships: sicknesses, the death of her sister and brother, and not being able to have children.

Gilbert expressed his idea of marriage in these words: "We are two in one." That expression underlined the kind of union proper to the institution of marriage: a deep and total union, an indivisible union of life. In addition he let himself be helped by his wife, which permitted him to evolve in his convictions and habits. He showed Frances that he needed her at every moment. This was very important for her, as shown by the commentary that she made after his death: "I almost can't bear to feel that he doesn't need me anymore."

Chapter 11

JACQUES MARITAIN AND RAÏSSA OUMANÇOFF (1904)

United in their search for the meaning of life, they found faith after they were married

Raïssa Oumançoff was born in Rostov, Russia, on September 12, 1883. When she was two years old, her family moved to Mariupol, a small port city on the Sea of Azov. She had a happy childhood, especially due to the care of an affectionate mother and her close relationship with her maternal grandfather, whom she always remembered for his kindness, gentleness, and piety. Her entrance into school at the age of seven increased her happiness:

> I entered into the world of knowledge. My heart beat with infinite hope. I was going to read and I believed that everything that was written was true. . . . Everything about school was a feast for me: the getting up early, challenging the snow and ice, when our neighbors did not take me in their sleigh. . . . There were in those days, in the neighborhood of the school, lots that were not yet built on, where one could see the first shoots of grass piercing the snow and announcing the coming of Spring. This sight,

after a long and rigorous winter, was one of the great joys of my childhood.[1]

Little Raïssa was much loved and praised by her teachers, who presented her to her classmates as an intelligent, studious, and good girl. This aroused bad will among the parents of her classmates, increased by the fact that she came from a Jewish family. Her parents, Orthodox Jews, emigrated to France in 1893 to free themselves from the discrimination that existed in their country and to seek better educational opportunities for Raïssa and her little sister Vera.

Exile in Paris

The move from a small Russian city to a large European city meant a difficult period of adaptation for the whole family.

> When did I begin to love Paris? I don't know just when: it happened little by little. An older person needs a lot of time to understand the soul and the language of a city, and with still greater reason, a girl who comes from so far because of her race and her place of birth. My first impression was of sadness. . . . We were only able to live in two rooms in a rather dark house which I found quite ugly; it was not our spacious house in Mariupol, it did not have a patio at the disposition of the children, nor flowers. . . . No, nothing more than sad rooms, a gray house, a narrow street. . . . My parents, who did not know a word of French when they left Russia, miraculously were able to adapt themselves.[2]

---

1. Raïssa Maritain, *Las Grandes Amistades* (Buenos Aires: Desclée de Brouwer, 1954), 16–17.

2. Raïssa Maritain, 25.

Raïssa and Vera were enrolled in a small public school for girls from six to twelve years old:

> When our Father, who had brought us, left us in the play-ground, we suddenly found ourselves very much alone and fearful; at that moment I felt for the first time that I was a foreigner, in a strange country. . . . I experienced a sense of depression, but that sensation did not last. I soon came to like my school as much as I had liked my school in Mariupol. The simplicity, the kindness of the teachers, the politeness of the girls who adopted me and gave me, as I believe, a kind of favored treatment, had the advantage of calming me and freeing me of any timidity. That was a great help for me, especially during the first two weeks of grave trial.[3]

Raïssa was a very good student, almost always the first in her class. Along with intelligence she put forth constant effort. She was very responsible for a ten-year-old and demanded a lot from herself for family reasons:

> I had as a motive to sustain my efforts and my zeal the feeling of a particular duty: I knew that my parents had left Russia, suffering the pain of exile, poverty, separation from loved ones whom they left behind and whom they would never see again. All of this for my sister and me, to assure the future of our studies and the conditions of a worthy and free life, protected from anti-Semitic harassment. Nothing seemed difficult to them nor too hard as long as it permitted me to study as I wished. They understood, before I could notice it, that that would be my life, the happiness of my life. . . . Therefore very soon there was united a vivid gratitude to my instinctive feelings of loyalty

---

3. Raïssa Maritain, 26–27.

toward them. I made an effort not to disappoint them, and I felt, as the first born, as though the responsibilities of the family rested on me in a certain way.[4]

When Raïssa and Vera turned twelve, they were admitted to the next level of schooling. Raïssa became familiar with classic French literature. She was enthusiastic about the writings of Racine and Corneille. At fourteen she began to have problems with respect to God:

> I asked myself whether God really existed. I recall very clearly that I reasoned thus: if God exists he is also infinitely good and powerful. But if he is good, how can he permit suffering? And, if he is omnipotent, how does he tolerate the evil ones? Then he is neither omnipotent nor infinitely good and, therefore, he does not exist. . . . This was a drama that began for me, and in that drama I found myself alone. My parents were no help to me. They had abandoned almost all of their religious practices and the influence of my grandparents was far away. Nevertheless, they preserved their faith in God; and did not believe that their daughter could really lose it; they lived in this certainty. And at school I did not find any religious teaching either.[5]

Raïssa meets Jacques Maritain at the Sorbonne

Raïssa was admitted to the Sorbonne University at the age of seventeen. She matriculated in the school of science. She was not so much interested in increasing her factual knowledge as she was in seeking truth:

---

4. Raïssa Maritain, 28–29.
5. Raïssa Maritain, 33.

I was only really seeking that of which I had need to justify life, something that seemed necessary for me so that life not be an absurd and cruel thing. I needed the joy of intelligence, of the light of certainty, of a rule of life founded on a truth without defect. . . . And I thought that the natural sciences were the key to all knowledge.[6]

Raïssa suffered one deception: None of the problems that concerned her regarding truth and human life were dealt with by those wise men who taught about the structure of the physical universe. They avoided every exercise of the intelligence that tried to elevate itself above the simple verification of facts. But Raïssa needed to know nature in another way—in its causes and its essence. As a consequence she lost confidence in those teachers at the Sorbonne who despised metaphysics.

During this time of disappointment, in 1900 she met a student who shared her interests and intellectual concerns. He invited her to take part in a student protest movement against the tsarist police's wrongful treatment of Russian socialist students. His name was Jacques Maritain. He was a year older than Raïssa and had been born into a Protestant family in Paris.

At the time they met, Jacques already had obtained his licentiate degree in philosophy from the Sorbonne and was studying for a degree in science, which is why he coincided with Raïssa in some courses. Both of them were opposed to the materialistic teaching of positivism that reigned in that university and felt an equal desire for metaphysical wisdom that their professors did not offer. They also shared the same passion for poetry, art, and social justice, but the passion

---

6. Raïssa Maritain, 43–44.

that most united them was addressing the problem of truth and finding the meaning of life. They felt it unbearable to imagine that life was only an absurdity, as was taught in the halls of the Sorbonne.

Their mutual attraction was immediate. As Raïssa wrote:

> Soon we became inseparable. . . . After classes he accompanied me home. We had to walk a long way. Our chats were interminable. . . . For the first time I was really able to speak about myself, to go out of my silent reflections to communicate them, to tell of my torments. For the first time I met someone who inspired me from the first moment with absolute confidence; someone I knew who would never deceive me; someone with whom, above all, I could understand myself well. Someone else had pre-established between us a supreme harmony, despite such great differences of temperament and origin.[7]

From Friendship to Courtship

From their initial friendship soon sprang mutual love. Raïssa felt attracted by the same desire for truth that Jacques had, to which he added more maturity, scientific knowledge, and experience than she had. Many years later Maritain spoke of what he felt on August 14, 1902. He had written it in his diary:

> Raïssa and I have clearly felt our truth, that of the two of us, when all is said and done. What has happened within is ineffable and divine. The absolute sincerity, the profound harmony of our souls has filled us with an endless bliss.

7. Raïssa Maritain, 45–46.

Life, our life, has appeared to us just as it should be, and in silence we have made irrevocable promises.[8]

Discovering Henri Bergson and León Bloy

The environment of pseudoscientific positivism, skepticism, and relativism that continued to reign at the Sorbonne was exasperating for those who, like Jacques and Raïssa, felt a love for the truth and a desire to discover it:

> This philosophy of the truth, this truth so ardently sought, so invincibly believed, was still not for us more than a kind of unknown God. We reserved for it an altar in our heart, we loved it ardently without knowing it; in advance we granted it all rights over us, over our life. But we did not know what it might be, we did not know the path and what the means were to attain it. . . . Until the unforgettable day in which we heard Bergson, this idea of the truth, this hope for unsuspected discoveries, had been for all who were waiting for it some light that was implicitly, or explicitly scorned.[9]

It was Charles Péguy, a prestigious Catholic writer that despised the positivistic teachers at the Sorbonne, who advised Jacques and Raïssa to attend classes given at the College of France by a philosopher who, without being a Christian, did believe in spiritual realities: Henri Bergson. The Sorbonne and the College of France were separated only by a street, but it was not easy to cross because of the prejudice and lack of trust that existed between the two institutions:

8. Jacques Maritain, *Notebook* (Bilbao: Desclee de Brouwer, 1967), 24.
9. Raïssa Maritain, 78–79.

"The one who made us cross the street, who had us pass from one house to the other, was the declared enemy of the Sorbonne historicism: Charles Péguy."[10]

Jacques and his now fiancée Raïssa became habitual participants in Bergson's classes, which demonstrated that, by intuition, the human being is capable of arriving at the absolute. This description coincides with that which Jacques made in one of his books:

> The scientist and phenomenist philosophy of my teachers at the Sorbonne led me to despair of reason. At a certain moment I came to believe that I could find integral certainty in the sciences. Felix Le Dantec thought that I would be a disciple of his biological materialism. My greatest debt to my studies of that time in the School of Science was my meeting, not with Le Dantec, but with Raïssa, whom since that time I have had the joy of counting on in all my work in a perfect and healthy communion. Bergson was the first who responded to our deep desire for metaphysical truth, and who awakened in us the feeling of the Absolute.[11]

After the couple discovered Bergson, they were introduced to Catholic writer León Bloy, who showed them the beauty of holiness. Jacque and Raïssa had many prejudices against Catholicism; they considered it the religion of the rich. When León Bloy met them, he did not use apologetics with them but instead advised them to read lives of the saints. That experience removed the prejudice that the couple had towards Catholicism, and they realized it was

---

10. Raïssa Maritain, 77.

11. Jacques Maritain, *Confesión de Fe* (Paris: Editions de la Maison Francaises, 1941).

the religion of love, peace, freedom, and justice. León also showed them the personal witness of a faith deeply lived, even while being very poor.

> Bloy placed us before the fact of holiness, simply because he loved us. . . . He showed us heroic Catholicism, holiness in its terrible trials, in its humility and its divine charity in its asceticism, in the bliss in which it is realized, in its pure harmony, in its power, in its beauty.[12]

Wedding Bells Sound

In 1902 Jacques and Raïssa commit themselves to marriage:

> We were dating for two years at least when we decided to get married without waiting for the completion of Jacques' studies. Our wedding took place in the simplest way, without any "declaration." We were alone in the living room of my parents. Jacques sat on the floor next to my seat; it suddenly seemed to me that we had always been one next to each other and that we would be so forever. Without thinking about it I ran my hand over his head, he looked at me, and it was clear to us. The feeling that always—to my happiness and salvation, my life would be linked to that of Jacques spread in me. . . . Since that time our agreement was perfect and irrevocable.[13]

Shortly thereafter Raïssa was gravely affected by a throat problem. She had to undergo emergency surgery in very precarious medical conditions by the light of an oil lamp. With her return to health came a renewed joy of living. The

---

12. Raïssa Maritain, 135–137.
13. Raïssa Maritain, 95.

couple made preparations for their civil wedding, which was celebrated on November 26, 1904. In February 1906 Raïssa contracted another grave sickness, and Jacques—in great anguish—prayed on his knees and offered to accept Catholicism in exchange for her cure. León Bloy asked Raïssa to pray, putting a medal of Our Lady around her neck.

Raïssa recovered and, after talking it over with Jacques, told Bloy they both wanted to be baptized. On June 11, 1904, they were baptized as Catholics, along with Raïssa's sister Vera, at the Church of St. John the Evangelist in Paris. A few days later Jacques and Raïssa were married in a religious ceremony.

United in Marriage in the Face of Misunderstandings, Sickness, and Poverty

On August 25, 1906, Raïssa and Jacques left for Heidelberg to study biology for two years with Hans Driesh, with a scholarship from the Michonis Legacy. There Raïssa became gravely ill once again and asked for the anointing of the sick. At Bloy's suggestion they prayed to Our Lady of La Salette, and Raïssa's cure was very rapid. In June 1908 they returned to Paris. When they informed their parents that they had both converted to Catholicism, they discovered they had already learned this through the indiscretion of a friend and were very upset. Her parents considered the conversion a betrayal of the Hebrew race; his parents considered it a betrayal of the progress connected with the Third French Republic, a persecutor of Catholicism.

The Maritains moved, along with Raïssa's sister Vera, into an apartment on the Rue des Feuillantines. Returning to Paris meant living the experience of a happy marriage in the midst of poverty. Raïssa remembered it thus:

It was then that we faced for ourselves the first serious problem in the practical order. The time had come for Jacques to take on a philosophy teaching position in one of the state high schools, a right that he had because of his degree as a licentiate. But we were in a period of such violent anticlericalism, and, with reason or without it, facing the fear of not having complete freedom to teach in accord with his own convictions as a Christian and a philosopher—or of a Christian philosopher, if you prefer—we were completely without income. We were happy living without any secure income, although we had to earn a living.[14]

Jacques obtained work for an orthographic dictionary, which kept him occupied for a year. After this he worked on a dictionary of practical life, a position he held for three years. During that period he had a spiritual director, Fr. Clerissac, who suggested that he read St. Thomas Aquinas. Jacques was greatly impacted by studying the *Summa Theologica*, to the point of discovering fully his philosophical vocation.

Jacques Maritain's Lay Apostolate

From 1910 on, Maritain developed his Christian apostolate, which was based on Thomistic philosophy and would last for sixty years. This work expanded in 1912, when he became a philosopy teacher at the Lycée Stanislas. His goal was to introduce Thomistic thinking into secular culture, especially within the closed field of contemporary philosophy. He opened his eyes to the world of his time, without ever losing contact with the reality he lived as a Christian

---

14. Raïssa Maritain, 179.

thinker. Maritain's Catholicism was presented in his confer-
ences, articles, and books, as well as in the testimony of his
private life. He was a man of prayer. In 1913 he published
his first book: *Bergsonian Philosophy*, and was appointed asso-
ciate professor of the History of Modern Philosophy at the
Catholic Institute of Paris.

Their Works Can Be Considered as One

What Maritain produced would not have been possible
without the company and support of Raïssa. She was at his
side during their student era, she converted to Catholicism
with him, and she was his faithful wife to the end of her life.
Her name remains tied to that of her husband.

The relation between Jacques and Raïssa was so profound that their works can be considered as one. Jacques
wrote sixty books, but a great part of his thought was the
fruit of Raïssa's spiritual experience. Raïssa, from the secondary place where she wanted to remain, was the inspiration of
all of his work and the coauthor of some of their books, as
well as being the author of twelve of her own books. Along
with his spiritual director, she prompted Jacques to study St.
Thomas Aquinas.

One of Raïssa's greatest works was *We Have Been Friends
Together*, where she tells how the Maritain couple met those
who exercised a decisive influence on their lives—among
them Charles Péguy, Henry Bergson, and León Bloy. These
mentors helped them to discover the meaning of life when
they were students at the Sorbonne.

Between 1914 and 1940 Maritain produced a great
amount of work. Some of his books from that period are
his *Introduction to Philosophy, The Range of Reason, Integral
Humanism,* and *An Essay on Christian Philosophy.*

Exile in America

World War II surprised the Maritains, who were giving classes in Toronto and New York at the time. After the occupation of France by the German army and the formation of the Vichy government, they decided to remain in the United States, above all to preserve Raïssa from the persecution the Jews were experiencing in Europe. They took an apartment on Fifth Avenue in New York City.

Raïssa reflected on the sorrow produced by their exile:

> July 6, 1940. There is no more future for me in this world. For me life ended with the catastrophe which has submerged France in sorrow, and the world with her, at least all that in France and in the world is united to the human and divine values of free intelligence, of wise freedom, of universal charity. After a long time, perhaps never, our eyes will once more see our beloved France. Perhaps we will never again in this world see again those who are dearest to us above all. . . . Paris, Oh, beloved city whose name I can't write without profound nostalgia, without immense sorrow; oh, city that perhaps I will never see again, which perhaps I have abandoned forever! You who have nourished my soul with truth and beauty, you who gave me Jacques and my godfather Leon Bloy, and so many precious friends, who made the days of our life in you beautiful. Oh city of great suffering and of great love![15]

During that period, which lasted five years, Maritain gave classes in the universities of Princeton and Columbia and wrote several books denouncing the anti-Christian ideology of Fascism and Nazism: *Through the Disaster,*

---

15. Raïssa Maritain, 9, 24.

Christianity and Democracy; The Twilight of Civilization; The Rights of Man and Natural Law; Principles of a Humanist Politics; and *From Bergson to St. Thomas Aquinas.*

The Return to Europe

On November 10, 1944, contrary to what Raïssa had supposed, the Maritains were able to return to France, thanks to the defeat of Nazism. The merits acquired by Jacques during the war led Charles De Gaulle to appoint him ambassador of France to the Holy See. When Maritain presented his credentials, Pope Pius XII said to him, "We appreciate and salute in Your Excellency a man who making open profession of his Catholic Faith and of his devotion to the philosophy of the Common Doctor, has put his rich qualities at the service of the great doctrinal and moral principles that above all in these times of universal disorder, the Church never ceases to inculcate in the world."

Pius XII identified with Maritain's thought and greatly valued his work redefining and explaining Thomism. During Maritain's stay in Rome (1944–1948), he attended Mass every day in the pope's private chapel and received Communion from his hands. In 1948 he gave up his position as ambassador in order to have more time for his intellectual and apostolic work. From that year on he published many of his most important philosophical works.

Raïssa's Death and a Loving Husband's Grief

On November 4, 1960, Raïssa died after fifty-five years of intense and faithful married union. It was a very hard blow for Jacques since he lost his lifelong companion. Her remains were buried in Kolbsheim, France. Only after this sad event did Jacques discover the private diaries of his wife, and he was deeply impressed by the spiritual depth that until then had been hidden. Those documents revealed the author's intense life of prayer and her vocation as a contemplative in the middle of the world.

Maritain published two books with texts by his wife: *Contemplation on the Street* and *Raïssa's Journal*. He also clearly recognized Raïssa in two of his last books: *Carnet de Notes* and *The Peasant of the Garonne*. In *The Peasant of the Garonne*, he wrote the following:

> I want to mention, among the unmerited gifts that I have received from God, the greatest: to have shared for nearly 55 years, since our baptism, the life of two blessed beings, Raïssa and her sister Vera, who, in the midst of the tribulations of a very agitated life, were, without faltering for an instant, faithful to contemplative prayer, and totally dedicated to a union of love with Jesus, a love of his Cross and to the work that, through similar souls, he carries out in the midst of men. They taught me what contemplation in the world is. I was a latecomer, a worker of the intellect, thus exposing myself to believe certain things because my head understood them a little and because my philosophy lectured about them. But I was taught, and well taught, by the experience, the sorrows and the light of those two faithful souls. This is what animates me to try to render them homage in speaking here of things that surpassed me, although knowing that I was taught by example does not make it easier to translate into ideas and words what I learned there.[16]

Maritain intensified his contemplative life in his final years, but without ignoring the problems of society. From

---

16. Jacques Maritain, *The Peasant of the Garonne* (Bilbao: Desclée de Brouwer, 1967), 257–258.

a Christian point of view, he was a great interpreter of the times in which he lived.

In 1963 he was awarded the Grand Prize of Letters in France. Two years later Pope Paul VI asked him to come to St. Peter's Square in Rome and receive publicly the proceedings of the Second Vatican Council on behalf of the intellectuals of the Christian world. The decree on religious freedom included many of the philosopher's ideas that earlier had been accused of being heretical.

Maritain exercised his lay apostolate in the way recommended by the Council: through the example of his life and dispensing oral and written messages. On April 28, 1973, he died in Toulouse, France, at the age of ninety-one. On May 2, he was buried next to his wife in Kolbsheim in Alsace, near the German border.

■ ■ ■

The Early Stage of Maritain's Marriage

The Notebook of Jacques Maritain, published in 1965, lets readers know about the first years of his married life. On October 28, 1906, during the Maritains' stay in Heidelberg during the second year of their marriage, he wrote in his diary about those personal qualities of Raïssa that made him fall in love with her and which he continued to admire:

> Kindness, Purity. Raïssa always goes to the end, with an upright intention and with all her will. In her courage there is no calculation, nor defense in her piety. Where there is no beauty she suffocates and cannot live. She has always lived for the truth; she has never resisted the truth. She has never put difficulties before her spirit nor lied about her pain. She

always gives without keeping anything back. What is important to her heart as to her understanding is the essential reality; nothing that is just an accessory can make her vacillate. Her thought, her talent is always directed to the intuition. Since all of this is interior, it is all free. Her reason can only be satisfied by the real, her soul only by the absolute.[17]

Another of Maritain's annotations in his diary, made on June 20, 1907, expressed very well their relationship during the third year of married life:

Raïssa brought me to Schloss, beneath the beautiful green trees, whose shade is a paradise of freshness where one submerges oneself like a good swimmer in the waves. The joy of going along with my dear friend, like two good spouses who are spending a holiday among these bourgeois people in their Sunday best. My heart trembles seeing Raïssa so tender and so good.[18]

The Growth of Mutual Love in the Autumn of Marriage

Raïssa's Journal, published by Jacques in 1966, offers valuable information about the last years of their marriage. In January 1936 Raïssa wrote some words "to Jacques" in Meudon that express in a passionate way both her disposition to love him better, as well as her need to continue being loved:

Continue loving me so, I need a lot of love to live, and I know that I should love "as not loving," in the sense of St. Paul, and beyond the sense of St. Paul. What a terrible

---

17. Jacques Maritain, *Notebook*, 44.
18. Jacques Maritain, *Notebook*, 53.

vocation! For this reason God has placed next to me your marvelous tenderness. With whom would I have been able to live such a vocation if not with you? And, from now on, in an extraordinary alienation from all knowledge.[19]

On January 25, 1944, during their exile in New York, in her diary Raïssa included a fragment of a letter directed to Jacques. They contained words of consolation and a desire for happiness in the face of a setback suffered by her husband:

> If there is anything in this world that I cannot stand it is that you feel miserable. I desire with all my heart that that "moment of sadness" that inspired your letter of Saturday morning, has only been a moment. You have been the victim of an overwhelming illusion, because in the instability and insecurity of our lives, there is nothing you're responsible for. . . . These disappointments have been numerous in our lives, they are our part of the cross of Jesus, and in the depth of our soul we have never rejected them. I hope that God grants us the grace of supporting them better and better with the progress of life towards death and, finally, towards life with God. . . . In what refers to our life, to my life with you, I give thanks to God with all my soul. He has granted me a marvelous good fortune, the best that he could have destined me for. Together with you I have found all of the sweetness and light of which I had and have need. I have had the first fruits and the sweetest part of this light. And your love has always surrounded me, comforted me, given value to life. I know that you are also happy, dear Jacques, as much as it is possible in this world. Take courage, my dear. We are of those who have conquered the world.[20]

---

19. Jacques Maritain, *Notebook*, 219.
20. Jacques Maritain, *Notebook*, 219.

Chapter 12

❧

ANTONIO MACHADO AND LEONOR IZQUIERDO (1909)

A love that overcame the barriers of age and sickness

Antonio Machado was born on July 26, 1875, in Seville. Although he left that city when he was only eight, he had lasting memories linked to a happy childhood—with just a few incidents he preferred to forget, as he mentioned in one of his writings. Not only the landscape of Seville but the people he knew there remained a permanent theme in his poetry.

Antonio was the second of five children in a family characterized as "liberal." He confessed to having in his veins "drops of Jacobin blood" and a deeply rooted Spanish-style republicanism.[1]

His father, Antonio Machado Alvarez, was a lawyer with a degree in arts. He published studies of Andalusian and Galician folklore and collaborated with the "republican" press, and he influenced his children with his love of literature.

---

1. Ian Gibson, *Ligero de equipaje. La vida de Antonio Machado* (Madrid: Aguilar, 2006), 405.

The image of his admired father was always a vivid one for Antonio. He never forgot the verses his father taught him or the hunting trips they took together. The family lived in a section of a palace rented from the Duke and Duchess of Alba. In their home there was a marked "progressive" atmosphere that influenced the education of the children. There were frequent gatherings of intellectuals and artists moderated by his grandfather.

Machado's Youth in Madrid

In 1883 Antonio's grandfather became a professor at the Central University of Madrid, and the whole family moved to the Spanish capital. Antonio continued his elementary schooling at the Free Institute of Education, where his brother Manuel was also enrolled. In 1893, when he was eighteen, his father died of tuberculosis. As a result, his family's financial problems forced him to interrupt his studies several times.

Antonio made his first trip to Paris in 1899, where his brother Manuel, now a poet, was living. Later Antonio worked with him as a playwright. In Paris he worked as a translator and became acquainted with other writers, such as Oscar Wilde. In 1900 he did some acting and finished his secondary studies at the Cardinal Cisneros Institute of Madrid.

He made a second trip to Paris in 1902, and upon his return he published his first book of poetry, *Soledades*, which he wrote between 1899 and 1902. This work was well received by the intellectuals of the time, and from 1903 to 1906 he collaborated in Madrid with various periodicals and literary reviews. But the income from his poetic work was not sufficient to support the quality of life he desired. Therefore in 1906 he decided to make use of his knowledge of French. At age thirty-two he prepared for the examination to become a French teacher in a secondary school. He was successful, and the following year he was assigned to the Institute of Soria. In that same year he published with considerable success *Soledades, Galerias y Otros Poemas.*

Machado Discovers the City of Soria—and Leonor

Machado began teaching in Soria in 1907. After staying for a few months in temporary quarters, he moved to a boardinghouse run by Isabel Cuevas and her husband, Ceferino Izquierdo.

Thus the poet found himself teaching, a vocation to which he did not feel called, and living far from his beloved capital, which was the heart of the literary world. He was not prepared for the life of a teacher or life in a small provincial city. Therefore in the summer of 1908 when he heard there was a vacancy for a French teacher in the San Isidro Institute of Madrid, he communicated to the Ministry of Public Instruction that he wanted to take the examination for this post. But he did not, in fact, take the exam. The reason may be that he had fallen in love with Leonor Izquierdo Cuevas.

Leonor was the niece of Machado's landlady. Although she had been born in Almenar, a small village near Soria, she had lived in that boardinghouse since 1906. She met Machado on September 21, 1907, when she was only thirteen. Machado felt a true love for her, but there was a problem. He felt timid toward women, and he feared being rejected. And so he came up with the idea of declaring his love by means of a poem that he left for Leonor to see, through apparent carelessness. His objective was made clear in the last verses: *Y la niña que yo quiero, ay! preferirá casarse con un mocito barbero.* (And the girl that I love, alas! prefers to marry a young barber.)

Leonor did have a boyfriend who was a barber. But the girl—as well as her parents—preferred the poet. Why would she accept him in spite of his being twice her age? A possible motive is that Leonor was captivated by the culture and humanity of this stranger; another was that she was enchanted by poetry; and a third motive was that this young man had a disposition quite the opposite of her authoritarian and violent father. Surely Leonor saw him, at first, as the good and affectionate father she did not have.[2]

A Wedding Between Two People of Very Different Ages

After waiting for Leonor to reach the legal age for marriage (fifteen at that time), they were married on July 30, 1909, at ten in the morning in the Church of St. Mary Major in Soria. The ceremony was officiated by the chaplain of the Institute where Antonio taught. Antonio's mother and three of his brothers and sisters came from Madrid for the wedding.

On a happy day like that, the couple had to suffer some jeers from a group of young men because of their age difference (thirty-four and fifteen). For their honeymoon Antonio and Leonor took a train to Barcelona, but when they reached Saragossa, about 180 miles short of their destination, they found they could not continue because of a strike caused by a government decision to send reservists to fight in Morocco. They changed their plans and traveled instead to Fuenterrabia on the Atlantic coast of Spain not far from the French border, where they spent the summer.

2. Gibson, 207–214.

In the fall they returned to Antonio's apartment in Soria on the plaza of the Theatines. Antonio wrote intensely. He dedicated his free time to reading and walking. He got to know Soria with its fields and people, and through that, Castile.

Contrary to his first impression on arriving in Soria, he later confessed that his stay in that city was the most decisive and happy period of his life, since there he married the woman he adored and would never forget. Antonio and Leonor felt very united and happy in their marriage. They frequently walked along the banks of the Duero River, from San Polo, a Roman ruin of a fortified temple, to San Saturio, the shrine of the patron of the city. During this period the poet published his *First Proverbs and Songs* and worked hard on a book that when published would be entitled *Campos de Castilla.*

In October 1910, Machado made a strenuous excursion without Leonor to the source of the Duero at the summit of Monte Urbion, crossing rivers, lakes, and forests, about which impressive legends endure. One of them, told by a peasant farmer, inspired his work *La Tierra de Alvargonzalez,* which he wrote first in prose and later in verse.

A Second Honeymoon, Cut Short by Illness

In January 1911 Antonio and Leonor, who were still very much in love, realized their dream of visiting Paris together. The trip was financed by a scholarship from the Board of Advanced Studies. They stayed in a small hotel and there enjoyed a second honeymoon. Antonio updated his knowledge of historical grammar and Medieval French Philology. He also attended courses taught by Henri Bergson, a vitalist philosopher whom he greatly admired. And there was still time to finish writing *La Tierra de Alvargonzalez.*

Antonio toyed with a plan of spending the summer with Leonor in Brittany, but the plans were discarded when Leonor fell ill. On July 14 she vomited blood, a symptom of tuberculosis. A desperate Antonio went all over the city without finding a doctor because it was Bastille Day. The next day he brought Leonor to a hospital. There she remained for the whole summer, with her anxious husband at her bedside. In September the doctors authorized her release, but Antonio lacked financial resources to bring her back to Spain. He asked for help from his friend, the well-known poet Ruben Dario, and received the amount he needed. The couple reached Soria on the 20th of that month.

Leonora grew worse day by day. Antonio gave her a copy of his recent book *Campos de Castilla*, published in June 1912, which contained the dedication "To Leonorina of my soul" (*A mi Leonorina de mi alma*). At the end of July her final agony began, and on July 31 she received the last rites. Antonio held his wife's hands until the end. She died on August 1st and was buried in the municipal Catholic cemetery. On August 8, 1912, Antonio moved to Madrid in an attempt to overcome his sorrow and loneliness. He tried to obtain a professorship in that city, asking support from a prominent intellectual, Giner de los Rios, but he did not get the position.

From Soria to Baeza

On August 30, 1912, the Institute of Baeza, located in South Central Spain, announced a translation competition to fill the vacant post of French Language professor. Machado applied for this and won the competition. He arrived in Baeza on November 1st accompanied by his mother. That same year he published his book *La Tierra de Alvargonzalez*.

His first impression of Baeza was less than positive due to the people's apparent indifference and the hurtful class distinctions. Antonio rebelled against the mediocrity of the environment. He spoke of the spiritual superiority of the less affluent lands he had just left. Nevertheless he did not remain passive:

> He felt himself a prisoner in that atmosphere of tedium and monotony that he was breathing but he did not get tied up in himself. Antonio had decided that his life as a poet only had a raison d'être if it was involved in other people, and therefore he decided that he must get to know and understand those people, and those lands, that were new to him. Although the presence of Castile, and especially Soria, remained indelibly engraved in his thought, it would soften with time to the extent that he went more deeply into what now surrounded him. This period of his life, from 1912 to 1919, would be one of the most important in the life of our poet.[3]

Antonio gradually made contact with the ordinary people of Andalusia, thus beginning his commitment to a Spain that needed social change.

Machado Sees Himself as a Philosopher and a Poet

In May 1913, Machado sent his friend Juan Ramon Jimenez a brief autobiography for an anthology that was being prepared. Here are some excerpts:

---

3. M. Soriano, *Antonio Machado* (Madrid: Club Internacional del Libro, 2002), 49.

I do not have the vocation of teacher and much less that of a university professor. But I try to fulfill my duty. My lectures have been especially in philosophy and literature but I am a fan of all the sciences. . . . I have a great love for Spain and an idea of Spain which is completely negative. . . . Basically I am a believer in a spiritual reality opposed to the sensible world. I have a great aversion to all that I write, after it is written, and my greatest torture is to correct my compositions in the printing proofs. This explains why all of my books are plagued with *errata*. My great passion is for traveling. . . . I have never been a womanizer and all pornography disgusts me. I adored my wife and am not thinking of marrying again.[4]

Between 1913 and 1915 Machado contributed to various literary magazines. In 1915, at the age of forty, he began his studies in Liberal Arts at the University of Madrid as a non-matriculated student. In 1917 he met the young poet Federico Garcia Lorca from Granada, and that same year the first editions of his *Complete Poems* and *Selected Works* were published.

From Baeza to Segovia and Madrid

In 1919 Machado moved to Segovia as an *instituto* (preparatory school) teacher. The local press noted his arrival and republished some of his poems. He lived in a modest boardinghouse, which is now preserved as a museum. He would spend weekends in Madrid. In collaboration with some friends, he created the People's University in Segovia: a free and popular institution, open to people of all walks of life. During his stay

---

4. Gibson, 287–288.

in Segovia, he wrote for various magazines, and along with his brother Manuel, produced two theatrical works.

From 1928 until the beginning of the Spanish Civil War, he had a secret romantic relationship with a woman whom he called Guiomar in his poetry. In 1933 he moved to Madrid as a teacher at the Instituto Calderon de la Barca. He and his brother Manuel produced another theatrical work entitled *La duquesa de Benamejí*. Then in 1935 he became a professor at the Instituto Lope de Vega of Madrid.

In the summer of 1936, the situation in Madrid became very tense. The Nationalist forces were confronting those of the Popular Front, which supported the government. The "two Spains" that Machado had often spoken of were on the point of a civil war. That year Machado also received notice that his fellow poet Federico Garcia Lorca had died. Although he wanted to remain in Madrid, two writer friends of his advised him to leave the city.

From Madrid to Exile and Death in Collioure, France

On November 25, Machado—along with his mother and three brothers, José, Francisco, and Joaquin—left for Valencia. The Machado family found a place to live in the village of Rocafort, a few miles from Valencia in the country. Although his health was not good, Antonio continued to work. Some of his work expressed opposition to the Nationalist forces led by Franco. In March 1938 he moved to Barcelona with his mother and brother José. His brother Manuel, who lived in the Nationalist part of Spain, had by this time become one of the principal writers in support of Franco. In December of that year the Nationalists began an offensive against Catalonia, and the Republican authorities advised Machado to prepare to move to France. In January the family, with a government-provided auto, joined a caravan of vehicles heading for France.

Once they had crossed into France at the end of January, they had the good luck of not being sent to a camp for refugees (which were more like concentration camps), and through the efforts of a friend, the Spanish embassy in Paris agreed to provide for their expenses. They took a train to the small fishing village of Collioure and moved into a hotel.

By this time Machado was quite sick, and by the middle of February his heart began to fail. He died on February 22, 1939. His mother died just a few days later.[5]

■ ■ ■

Antonio Machado's Love for Leonor

Antonio Machado's love for Leonor is one that deserves a place in the best anthologies of love stories. It was an authentic love, one that developed over several months of daily contact: Their relationship overcame a substantial difference in their ages and the resulting social criticism; it resulted in his initial plan to leave Soria as soon as he could; and it gave origin to his most inspired verses. Machado defined his love for Leonor as "an Eros with wings," in contrast to the "Eros without wings" of his previous loves.

Through Abel Martín, one of Machado's fictional characters, we hear that the great incentive of love is not physical attraction but "the metaphysical thirst for what is essentially another." With this Machado is telling us that love should not be confused with instinct. Instinct is a mere physical or

---

5. Gibson, 611–628.

carnal attraction to the other. Love, on the other hand is attraction toward the entire person of the man or woman. If this were not so, there would be a depersonalization of the relationship between the man and woman: it would simply be a relationship of a man-object with a woman-object.

The essence of love is pleasure in the existence of a particular person, followed by the inclination toward and union with the good that existence encompasses. True love does not conform to sensible loving, with a love based solely on what the other has that is *specific and repeatable*—physical qualities captured by the external senses; instead it aspires to a personal encounter with the beloved as a *unique and unrepeatable* person. The person is loved in and for oneself, not for the pleasure or utility he or she can provide.

Machado's love poems that refer to Leonor never express any erotic passion, but instead are about deep feelings: affection, loneliness, sorrow, melancholy, nostalgia. . . . Most of them are haunting and filled with lyricism.

In Antonio and Leonor's married life, love became a mutual partner. We see this in their frequent walks along the banks of the Duero River and their second honeymoon trip to Paris. The fact that Antonio and Leonor shared a taste for poetry also helped provide an intense and enriching life together for both of them.

Antonio's Sacrificial Love

When Leonor was admitted to the hospital in Paris, Antonio did not leave her bedside. And when, after a brief improvement, she had a relapse with the arrival of the cold winter in Soria, Antonio abandoned everything to care for her with great tenderness, hoping that she would survive until the arrival of spring:

She needed to breathe pure air and Antonio, walking heavily, pushed a small cart each day towards the shrine of Mirón. There he rented a little place where they could take refuge when it rained. When they returned to his apartment in the Plaza of the Theatines, Antonio remained constantly next to the young patient and took care of her lovingly. From that very sad epoch came one of his most moving poems entitled: "A un olmo seco" ("To a Dried Oak"); a torn attempt at hope on the part of the poet who still trusts in an impossible miracle.[6]

The verses of the poem express an ambivalent feeling of anxious hope: From the old elm, split by lightening and half rotten, a few green leaves have sprouted with the rain of April and the sun of May.

That episode exemplifies perfectly that to love calls for giving oneself in self-surrender, giving of one's own life and renouncing what is one's own.[7] It also lets us see that the giving required in marriage is not partial, but total, and not limited by time:

Authentic human love is, like the divine, a giving and surrender of one person to another. Love is, in a certain sense, the going out of oneself to live for the other. Therefore the great obstacle for marriage and the family is the same thing that is an obstacle for love itself: egoism, which leads one to center on oneself, to close in on oneself, to live for oneself. Thus in marriage we cannot say people love one another just because they live together. Nor is love simply giving something, for example, one's own body in the conjugal relationship, because loving is not "giving things,"

6. Soriano, 44.
7. Alejandro Llano, La Vida Lograda (Barcelona: Ariel, 2002), 180–184.

but giving one's entire person, and the giving is entire when one gives oneself totally and forever, therefore love is indissoluble. Not to put personal surrender at the base of love is to rest it on shifting sand and in that way one cannot build anything solid.[8]

Sorrow and Unending Nostalgia for a Lost Love

The hoped-for miracle did not come. Leonor's death plunged her husband into a deep depression. Antonio expressed his great sorrow in deeply felt verses:

> Lord, you have torn from me what I loved most. Listen once
>   more, my God, to the cry of my heart.
> Your will be done, O lord, against my own.
> Lord, now we are alone, my heart, and the sea.

> (Poem CXIX)

The remembrance of what they had experienced together helped Antonio to continue living spiritually with Leonor. He expressed his feelings in a letter to his admired teacher Miguel de Unamuno:

> The death of my wife has left my spirit torn apart. My wife was an angelic creature cruelly cut short by death. I adored her; but above love there is piety. I would have preferred a thousand times to die myself rather than see her die. I would have given a thousand lives for hers. I don't think there is anything extraordinary in this feeling of mine. There is something immortal in us that wants to die with the one who dies. Perhaps this is the reason that God came

---

8. Llano, 180–184.

into the world. Thinking of this consoles me somewhat. At times I have hope. . . .

While I fought at her side against the irremediable, I was sustained by the consciousness of suffering much more than she was, for she, when you get down to it, never thought about dying, and her sickness was not painful. After all, she now lives in me more than ever and at times I firmly believe that I am going to recover her. Patience and humility.[9]

The figure of the traveler is one often used by Machado. One who is walking holds a dialogue with the landscape while he goes in search of his goal.

Far away was the period of life (with Leonor) in the fields of Soria. Machado often walked, alone and on foot, the five miles from Baeza to Ubeda. On those walks he never lost his nostalgia for his lost love.

The memory of a lost love brings suffering, but it also keeps the heart alive. To suffer for love is preferable to forgetting and ceasing to suffer, because the heart that does not love is dead.

---

9. Gibson, 285–286.

Chapter 13

⅔

CHARLES OF AUSTRIA AND ZITA OF BOURBÓN-PARMA (1911)

A love unaltered by war and exile

Charles I of Habsburg-Lorraine was born on August 17, 1887, in the castle of Persenbeug on the banks of the Danube, some sixty miles from Vienna. He was the first son of Archduke Otto and Maria Josepha of Saxony, daughter of the last king of Saxony. He was married in 1911 to Princess Zita of Bourbón-Parma, who was five years younger. They would be married for eleven years before his death. Theirs was a union between two devout Catholics.

On June 28, 1914, after the assassination of his uncle, Archduke Franz Ferdinand of Habsburg-Lorraine, in Sarajevo, Charles became, much sooner than was considered likely, the heir of Emperor Franz Joseph I to the throne of the Austro-Hungarian Empire. Austria-Hungary was a great multiethnic empire that extended from the Adriatic Sea towards the center of Europe. In 1914 it covered some 260,000 square miles and had almost 53 million inhabitants. It was the second largest country in Europe in size and the third largest in population. As far as its economy was concerned, it ranked sixth in the world.

Charles ascended to the throne on November 21, 1916, upon the death of his elderly great-uncle, Franz Joseph I, taking the names Charles I of Austria and Charles IV of Hungary. The First World War was underway. He would be the last emperor of the Austro-Hungarian Empire.

Zita of Bourbón-Parma was born on May 9, 1892, in Villa Pianore, close to Viareggio, a city in the Italian province of Tuscany. She was the seventeenth child of Duke Robert I of Parma and his second wife, Maria Antonia de Braganza. Zita was the last empress and queen consort of Austria-Hungary. Charles and Zita had eight children.

Prince Charles' Childhood and Early Education

Charles's father, Otto, gave him a careful education that included physical training and languages. His mother, Maria Josepha, was very pious and dedicated to the education of her son. She gave him a deep religious education with the collaboration of a Dominican priest. She also had the help of Mlle. Liese, an extraordinary instructress whom Charles was very fond of.

In 1893 the family moved to the city of Sopron where Otto was appointed commander of the Ninth Regiment of Hussars. At a very early age Charles showed a generosity that later would become proverbial. For example, when he was given presents, he would give them to poor children. Charles received a strict military education from an early age and did not complain, despite his aversion to war.

The death of his grandfather, Karl Ludwig, in 1896 turned the young archduke into a potential heir to the throne. From that moment on Charles received a formation in accord with the requirements of a future ruler. Two years later the family left the small city of Sopron for Vienna, where Otto had been named a general.

Charles studied with Catholic teachers at the Scottish Lyceum of Vienna. He expanded his knowledge by traveling to different countries. Being very gifted in learning languages, he acquired a mastery of those spoken in the empire. On November 19, 1896, he made his first holy Communion and received a crucifix from his father that he kept for the rest of his life. In 1905 he began his military career, and two years later he officially came of age.

Charles and Zita Meet

Maria Teresa de Braganza, the third wife of Karl Ludwig, took great interest in the future marriage of her grandson Charles. After studying all the marriageable princesses of Europe, she reached the conclusion that the best suited was Zita, one of her brother-in-law Robert, Duke of Parma's daughters. This sixteen-year-old had all of the required conditions: ancestors, lineage, property, family, religion, spirituality, education, and beauty. In addition, her character, determined and resolute, would be of great help to Charles. Undoubtedly she had inherited her strength and character from her mother. Zita's formation was one of her strongest points, since she had received a good spiritual preparation and an excellent humanistic education.

Zita had been educated in different religious boarding schools. The last was that of the French Benedictine nuns of Solesmes on the Isle of Wight. The culture and the French environment enchanted her.

Zita clarified in an interview many years later that her first meetings with Charles were a series of coincidences. She knew him from her early years when they had shared children's games at her Aunt Maria Teresa's home.

In 1909 Charles was sent to the garrison in the city of Brandeis-sur-L'Elbe in Bohemia as captain of a battalion. Near there, in Franzensbad, Zita and her aunt Maria Teresa were spending a few days at a health resort. Thus Charles and Zita had the opportunity to get to know each other better. They were no longer children—he was twenty-two and she was seventeen. Soon thereafter they began their courtship.

Charles was quickly smitten, while for Zita it was just the beginning of a process: She fell in love with him little by little, over a period of two years.

Charles confided to his mother his desire to marry Zita. Maria Josepha advised him to wait, but the following year she assented and transmitted the petition for marriage to the king, which he accepted. The betrothal was celebrated in the chapel of the castle of Villa Pianore, on June 13, 1911. When the service ended, Charles said to his future wife: "Now we will help each other to reach heaven!"

Walking through the gardens of the castle, the betrothed had an especially intimate conversation. Charles felt a need to tell Zita exactly how his life had been, without omitting things of which he was ashamed. Then he asked her: "After what I have told you, are you willing to marry me?"

Charles promised to be faithful forever and swore that if he ever deceived her in anything, no matter how small, he would tell her about it before a day had gone by. After this they saw each more frequently. In the summer of 1911, they took a trip to various cities of Europe. It was a good occasion to get to know each other better and confirm their harmony of feelings and of intellect.[1]

---

1. José M. Cejas, *La Historia de Amor de Carlos de Austria y Zita de Borbon Parma*, *www.conelpapa.com/historiasdeamor.*

The marriage was planned in accordance with the traditions of Austrian etiquette. Charles asked his fiancée to go to Rome to request an audience with Pope Pius X, along with an apostolic blessing for the two of them. Zita went with her mother and was received in a private audience. "May God bless you, my dear daughter," said the pope. "I am happy about this marriage. May your country and that of the future monarch benefit from this blessing."

The pope promised Zita that he would delegate his marriage blessing through one of his prelates.

The Wedding and First Years of Married Life

Charles and Zita each made separate retreats before their marriage. The ceremony was celebrated on October 21, 1911, at one of her family's estates: it took place in the chapel of the Castle of Schwarzau, located in lower Austria, close to the Alps. Charles wore the uniform of a Cavalry captain, Zita a diadem given to her by Franz Joseph and a veil bordered with the fleur-de-lis of the Bourbon royal house.

Cardinal Bisletti read the sermon written by the pope. At the end of the ceremony, he congratulated them and gave them the text of the homily, privately mentioning that he had omitted a phrase where the pope greeted Charles and Zita as the future sovereigns of the monarchy. Pius X's prophecy was fulfilled three years later with the assassination of the heir to the throne, Franz Ferdinand, in Sarajevo.[2]

The newly married couple spent their first month at the Villa Wartholz, one of the imperial castles in lower Austria.

---

2. Michel Dugast, *Carlos de Habsburgo, El Ultimo Emperador* (Madrid: Palabra, 2005), 31.

Then they made a pilgrimage to the Shrine of Mariazell to ask protection from Our Lady. After this they began their honeymoon.

After his return to Vienna, Charles rejoined his Dragoons regiment in Bohemia. Shortly thereafter the regiment was transferred to the city of Kolomea in the Carpathian Mountains for a period of maneuvers. Charles and Zita spent this time in a modest chalet. A long and cold winter awaited them, but there they lived one of the happiest stages of their life together.

With the maneuvers over, they returned to Vienna and were present at the International Eucharistic Congress celebrated there in September 1912. On November 1, Charles was named commander of the first battalion of the 39th infantry regiment in Vienna. On the 20th of that same month his first son, Otto, was born.

The following year the family moved into the Hetzendorf Palace, ceded to them by Emperor Franz Joseph. Charles, as an instructor of officers, formed his students and motivated them by his example. He followed his usual ascetical life, characterized by moderation and frequent fasts.

At the beginning of 1914, little Otto was joined by a sister, Adelaide. Later there came seven more children between 1915 and 1922. One of them, the Archduke Rudolf, born in 1919, gave a brief sketch of his father in the prologue to the biography written by Michel Dugast:

> He was a deeply pious man, a faithful husband, an excellent father of seven children plus the one that my mother was expecting, an expert army officer, a notable Chief of State with an extraordinary memory, a very hard worker, strong and prudent. He was a very good spouse to my mother, herself an energetic and active person, of great foresight and deeply in love with her husband. Both loved

their countries and their inhabitants. They did everything they could to obtain peace and the welfare of their peoples. At the end of the war they were expelled from their country, had all of their property confiscated, and were forced to take a ship to Madeira, where, without a cent, my father died as a result of pneumonia and a heart attack. The cause was the incredible stress provoked by the enormous efforts he made throughout his reign. The Holy Father and the Church saw to it that those heroic efforts for his people and for the Church were recognized before the world on October 3, 2004 in St. Peter's Square.[3]

The Crime in Sarajevo

The heir to the empire, Archduke Franz Ferdinand (Charles's uncle), had married a commoner and therefore his children could not inherit the throne. This meant that at his death Charles would become emperor. At the beginning of 1914 he invited Charles and Zita to his residence, the Belvedere Palace. There the following dialogue took place:

— I am convinced that I am going to be assassinated. The police know about it.

— Uncle, you are too pessimistic. We have a competent police force.

— That's true, but there are assassinations that one cannot prevent. If they kill me, I would like you to take care of Sofia and my child, as executor of my will. After my death my lawyer will give you my will. But not a word in front of Sofia, she would worry too much.[4]

3. Dugast, 12.
4. Dugast, 36.

On June 28, 1914, the people of Sarajevo in Bosnia were awaiting the archduke's visit, accompanied by his wife. When the motorcade was near the "Appel Quay," an explosion was heard. A bomb thrown by a Serbian conspirator was thrown into the archduke's car. But Franz Ferdinand had the coolness to grab the device before it exploded and throw it out of the car. The motorcade continued driving through the city, but with a change of route. Suddenly the car at the head made a sudden turn and went along the original route. At that moment a man with a pistol ran up to the car and shot Sofia and Franz Ferdinand. Both died a few minutes later.

On the following day Charles went to meet his uncle, Emperor Franz Joseph, who was returning from a trip and was deeply shaken. As the new heir, Charles received the remains of the two victims of Sarajevo in the South Station of Vienna. On July 6 he led the burial procession to the crypt of the chapel of the Artstetten Palace.

Suddenly a tremendous burden had fallen on him: He was the direct heir to the crowns of Austria, Hungary, and Bohemia.

Austria Declares War on Serbia— The First World War Begins

On July 7 the Royal Council gathered, presided over by Emperor Franz Joseph, to consider Austria's response to Serbia for the assassination in Sarajevo. Charles was not invited to the meeting because he was known to be a pacifist. The Council agreed to send an energetic ultimatum to Serbia, demanding an investigation of the assassination and an end to anti-Austrian propaganda. A response was demanded in forty-eight hours. But Serbia would not accept the idea of sending Austrian police to collaborate in the investigation, possibly because there were accomplices of the assassins in Serbia. As a consequence the Austrian ambassador immediately left Serbia.

Franz Joseph hesitated, but he finally agreed to sign a declaration of war, which was communicated to Belgrade on July 27th. Serbia was joined by Russia, France, Britain, and Italy, while Austria-Hungary was joined by Germany. The Sarajevo assassination thus brought about the beginning of the First World War.

On that day, Charles was appointed colonel of the first regiment of Hussars. On arriving at Hetzendorf, he was surprised that the majority of the people wanted the war. He was opposed to it, in spite of being an officer. On Franz Joseph's recommendation, he visited the principal cities of the empire for the purpose of promoting the mobilization of the armies. Charles was assigned to the general staff of Archduke Frederick, who was in command of military operations in Galicia. Before leaving for the front, he asked his wife to have the following words engraved on his sword: *Sub tuum praesidum confugimus, sancta Dei genitrix* (We fly to your protection, O Holy Mother of God).

At every moment he tried to diminish as much as possible the cruelty of the war. For example, he opposed a general who wanted to attack the Russians with gas, after the Austrians had been attacked in that way; he also prevented bombarding cities. On February 8 he traveled to Vienna to be present at the birth of his second son, Robert.

One of his military tasks was to carry out inspections, winning him the generals' friendship. Each morning at seven, he informed Franz Joseph of his activities. Before that time he had already attended Mass. Although he had a very heavy work agenda, he always found time to spend the evening with his family and explain the catechism to his children.

Franz Joseph's Death and Charles's Ascent to the Throne

In November 1916, Zita sent a telegram to her husband informing him that Franz Joseph was sick. Charles returned to Vienna immediately and, to avoid alarming the population, went to live with his family in the Wartholz villa. The health of the emperor became worse each day. He received a papal blessing transmitted by the nuncio of Benedict XV. He also went to confession and received Communion and the anointing of the sick with great devotion. He died on November 21, 1916, after a reign of sixty-eight years. On the following day, Charles and Zita attended a Mass celebrated for her great-uncle in the room where he died. They received Communion and prayed the Rosary together.

The death of Franz Joseph put Archduke Charles of Habsburg on the throne. At the age of twenty-nine, he found himself on a throne he had not sought in the midst of a terrible war involving almost all the nations of Europe. He inherited an empire in rapid decline. The new emperor issued a manifesto that included a clear reference to his search for peace:

> On asking heaven for grace and blessings for me and for my house, as well as for my beloved peoples, I swear before the All Powerful to administer faithfully the goods that have reached me through my ancestors. I will do all that is within my possibility to banish as quickly as possible the horrors and sacrifices that the war has brought and to return to my people the benefits of peace.

From the first moment of his reign, he openly opposed the war and tried to take the Austro-Hungarian Empire out of it, moved both by his personal convictions and by the economic situation of the participating countries, which was very worrying. He also proposed fighting against corruption, reestablishing a constitutional system in the monarchy, and maintaining the unity of the empire.

Charles, accompanied by Zita, received the crown of St. Steven during a ceremony on December 30, 1916, in the Church of Our Lady of Budapest. Thus he expressed the conviction that his position came from God. On his return to Vienna he learned of the negative response of the enemy countries to his proposal of peace of December 12.

Charles frequently went to the front, where he helped the wounded and had Mass celebrated, in spite of the disapproval of his retinue and the court. In the midst of the war, he found time to take care of his children, giving them a Christian formation and making them conscious of the responsibilities that came with their high status. Zita never forgot that in the coronation ceremony she had been entrusted with the mission of helping her husband in whatever was necessary. In 1917, behind Germany's back, Charles tried to obtain a separate peace agreement with the countries at war through his brother in law, Prince Sixtus of Bourbón-Parma. But this proposal failed because of the breakdown of bilateral negotiations with France. Charles then had to travel to Germany to assure Wilhelm II of his loyalty as an ally. On August 1 of that year, Pope Benedict XV directed a call to the belligerents for the signing of peace, which was supported by Charles. He was not listened to.

Zita Visits the Wounded

Zita regularly visited those wounded in the war, consoling and assisting them. One of the hospitalized, a farm worker from Tyrol, mentioned one of those visits.

One day, during the war, I saw the empress herself appear in a hospital in Vienna without her coming being announced beforehand. She stopped before each of the beds. A poor sick person and myself were the last ones in the ward. When she came to me she asked about my health. I answered that I was better off than my wife, who had just had a child and had no way of living because she had no war pension, and that I in my condition was not able to help her. A few days later I received a letter from my wife; the pension had suddenly arrived.[5]

Zita's humanitarian work had begun as soon as she and Charles ascended to the throne. She visited the poorest sections of Vienna, helping abandoned children and the sick. Later she expanded that aid to the orphans and war widows.

Attempts to Save the Unity of the Empire Fail

To the successive failures on the fields of battle, as well as mass desertions, was added the internal crisis of the monarchy. Dugast gives an eloquent description of the grave situation after four years of war:

The year 1918 was a nightmare for the civilian population. The winter was cold and rigorous. Vienna was suffering from hunger. The lines before food stores were long and the trolleys did not run to save coal, while the flu was causing thousands of deaths. The signs of discontent were multiplying. It was not rare to see writings against the war in the streets of Vienna. A strike broke out in the Arsenal. In the Hungarian camps the soldiers called for an independent Hungarian army and demanded separation from

5. Dugast, 177.

Austria. In Budapest a secret committee of workers and soldiers had formed, similar to the Russian soviets. Before the phantasm of a revolution the police took measures to protect the imperial family.[6]

In 1918 the Czech deputies demanded the creation of an autonomous Czechoslovak State. They were supported by strikes and popular demonstrations that culminated in a large meeting of solidarity with the Russian revolution. In Vienna the Danubian fleet revolted. After the collapse of the Bulgarian front in September 1918, Charles carried out strong reform measures to attempt to save the empire, but without success.

On October 16, 1918, he presented a manifesto, "To my faithful Austrian peoples," in which he announced the conversion of the empire into a federal state that would share only a single head of state. This measure came too late. The national councils that had been fostered among the different nationalities opted to abandon the empire. On November 1, the last Crown Council met and agreed to sign an armistice.

Charles showed Zita the document before signing it. She advised him not to do it, because it seemed like an abdication, and she gave him courage to maintain his position.

> A sovereign cannot abdicate; he can be deposed, despoiled of his rights by force, but no one can oblige him to recognize that he has lost them. He can always recuperate them, according to circumstances with the passage of time. But abdicate, never, never. I prefer to die with you. Then, Otto will succeed us. And even if we all die, there will always be other Habsburgs.[7]

---

6. Dugast, 173.
7. Dugast, 208.

Charles renounced his position as head of state on November 11, 1918, but not his rights as head of the dynasty. He wanted to maintain the possibility that the Habsburg monarchy might survive with another member of the family. By his responsible behavior he made possible, at the end of the war, a transition to a new order without any civil war. But in spite of this, he was exiled from his homeland.

The Exile

In March 1919 Charles was deposed by the Austrian parliament. On March 23, after assisting at Mass with his family and his retinue, the exile began. Dressed in the uniform of a field marshal, he took a train to Switzerland. On March 24 he protested in writing against his expulsion, approved on November 11 by the government and parliament.

Two years later in an attempt to prevent the establishment of Communist power in Central Europe, Charles tried to restore the monarchy in Hungary. The attempt failed and he was arrested and sent into exile on the Portuguese island of Madeira.

Charles and Zita and their children were forced to live in relative poverty in a very humid house. In March 1922 Charles suffered a respiratory ailment, diagnosed as double pneumonia, from which he did not recover. In his biography, Dugast wrote that Charles accepted his illness without complaint, forgiving those who had abandoned him, as a sacrifice for the peace and unity of his peoples. On his deathbed he recalled the motto of his life: "My whole commitment is always, in all things, to know as clearly as possible and follow the will of God, and this in the most perfect way."

He asked for confession and the anointing of the sick. In the midst of his sufferings, he prayed without rest, accompanied by Zita. These were his last words: "Lord, Thy will be done; I offer my life in sacrifice for my people; Sacred Heart of Jesus, I trust in you; Jesus, Mary, and Joseph."

A non-believing doctor who was assisting him felt so moved by his exemplary death that he converted. Charles died on April 1, 1922, at the age of thirty-five, and was buried in Madeira.

Zita's Faithfulness

Zita became a widow at the age of twenty-eight. She took charge of her large family and moved to Spain. She and her oldest son, Otto, became symbols of the unity of the exiled dynasty. She remained faithful to her husband's memory for the rest of her long life. She died in Zizers, Switzerland, on March 14, 1989, at the age of ninety-seven, spending her last years in a cloistered convent. The Austrian government gave permission for her to be buried in the crypt of the Capuchin monastery in Vienna with the other members of the Imperial House of Habsburg.

The Beatification of Charles of Austria

On April 1, 1972, on the fiftieth anniversary of his death, Charles's sepulcher was opened, and his body was found to be incorrupt. On October 3, 2004, the last Catholic emperor of modern history was beatified by Pope John Paul II. The pope called him "a friend of peace." In his homily at the Mass of beatification, John Paul II said the following:

> The fundamental task of a Christian consists in seeking in everything the will of God, recognizing it and following it. Charles of Austria, chief of state and a Christian, confronted this challenge every day. The war seemed to him to

be "something horrible." In the tumult of the First World War he tried to promote the initiative of peace of my predecessor Benedict XV. From the beginning, Emperor Charles I conceived of his task as a holy service to his people. His principal concern was to follow the vocation of a Christian to holiness also in his political action. For him, social assistance was important for this. May he be an example for all of us, above all for those who today have political responsibility in Europe!

▪ ▪ ▪

Charles and Zita's Surprising Maturity

Usually the beginning of falling in love is an idealized love with little basis in reality. It is subject to a certain deception with respect to what the person loved is like. Each one appears to be what he or she is not; one shows oneself as better than one is, in order to please the other. To this one unites the mutual desire for self-deceit: The person loved is imagined, more than known, according to one's own dreams. The emotional typically predominates over the rational.

This period of loving immaturity is not seen in the courtship of Charles and Zita. They give the impression that they both acted with head and heart. Each one made an effort from the beginning to know the other in a real way. And after knowing each other, they accepted each other fully, including their defects. Their courtship had four key moments: their meeting in the health spa of Franzensbad; the commitment ceremony; the intimate conversation they shared in the gardens of the Pianore palace; and the joint trip through Europe.

When they met at the spa, they must have had lots of personal conversation, for the definitive result was their falling in love. The fact that it was, for Charles, a love at first sight gave the relationship a touch of sane romanticism. It was not a matter of simple physical attraction or a mere emotional harmony, but pleasure at the good that existed in Zita as a person. It was not yet self-giving love, but a basis for it to arise.

Their courtship was not an end in itself; it was not an adventure or a passion but a means to determine if they were suited to each other with a view to a possible marriage. Mutual love evolved and matured, as one might expect at that stage:

> In courtship there is a point of departure: the physical and emotional attraction that arises from the first encounter: I like this woman (or this man). This is not yet love. The person in love should then further consider the question of giving oneself and receiving something more than oneself; a desire of self-giving that has to be mutual. Personal love arises: I am attracted by, or in love with, not only the physical qualities of the other, but with their spiritual, intellectual, and moral qualities, the whole person. I like the way he, or she, is, including their defects, which one will inevitably discover in a period of continued contact.[8]

During that courtship there soon emerged an outline for married life, a mutual and enthusiastic plan of a shared life. Charles and Zita knew it was necessary to formulate a plan

---

8. Amadeo Aparicio, *Casarse: Un Compromiso para Toda la Vida* (Pamplona: EUNSA, 2002), 81–83.

for a marriage commitment that would last forever. Later they would prove to be loyal to this plan.

The religious ceremony of their betrothal spoke itself of the fact that this marriage was for love and commitment—and that as Christians the contract was not just between two, but three: he, she, and God. In this sense Charles's comment to his future wife was significant: "Now we are going to help each other get to heaven!"

That mutual help is one of the ends of marriage. And the best help is not the material but the spiritual: that which contributes to making the other happy in this life and the other. Charles and Zita knew that, for Christians, engagement implies a plan of love in which God is not foreign:

> If you are engaged to be married, God has a project of love for your future as a couple and as a family. Therefore, it is essential that you discover it with the help of the Church. . . . The period of engagement is a time of expectation and preparation that needs to be lived in purity of gesture and words. It allows you to mature in love, in concern, and in attention to each other; it helps you to practice self-control and to develop your respect for each other. These are the characteristics of true love that does not place emphasis on seeking its own satisfaction or its own welfare.[9]

The intimate conversation in the palace gardens shows that Charles and Zita's relationship was not superficial but focused on understanding and values and fidelity.

Charles courageously took the responsibility of opening the book of his life to his fiancée because he felt, with good reason, that she had a right to know fully the person

---

9. Benedict XVI, Message for 22nd World Youth Day, 2007.

she would marry, since she was going to share her whole life with him. On sincerely promising faithfulness to Zita, Charles established the principal basis for a happy married life. Engagement was also for them what it should be: a stage of responsible preparation for their future married life. This was confirmed by the fact that they each made a retreat beforehand.

A Good Start

The first thing the newly married couple did was to go on a pilgrimage to a Marian shrine, asking Our Lady's protection. The honeymoon trip could wait. By putting it in her hands, their marriage began well. They were conscious that married life is not easy and required both human and supernatural help.

Zita accompanied Charles to his new military destination in Kolomea. They spent a long, cold winter in a house without comforts far from Vienna. And they did so without any complaints. This shows the sacrificing, patient, and dedicated love of an exemplary wife. It would be the prelude to what happened during the rest of their married life. That winter in Kolomea was one of the happiest periods of their marriage. The difficulties that arose with the war only reinforced the couple's union. Let us recall, for example, that before leaving for the front, Charles asked his wife to have a beautiful invocation to our Lady engraved on his sword imploring her protection.

Zita Was the Perfect Wife for the Last Emperor

Maria Teresa of Braganza was right when, before the engagement, she commented that young Zita had all the qualities necessary to be empress and Charles's wife. Only a woman with her moral fortitude and energetic, active, and decided character could provide the support the last emperor would need throughout such a convulsed reign. Zita fulfilled what she promised in the coronation ceremony: to help her husband in all that might be necessary—which would be a lot.

Zita was always a devoted and faithful wife. She sacrificed her own well being, putting before it that of her husband and her children and the needs of her country. An example of this was her humanitarian work and her visits to the hospitals.

Her strong moral convictions were a key factor in the most difficult moments of their reign—for example, when she encouraged Charles not to sign the document of abdication. Her attitude was heroic, since by avoiding the abdication she proved she was ready to die with her husband.

With the passage of years, Zita's love and dedication increased. She loved her husband in sickness and in health, in power and in exile. She accompanied him during the difficult stay in Madeira and did not cease to pray with him.

After Charles's death, Zita took charge of her eight children and made a painful journey through several countries until finding refuge in Spain. She bore with dignity the sorrowful tragedy of her people and her family and stayed faithful to the memory of her husband until the end of her days.

Chapter 14

❧

André Maurois and Jeanne-Marie de Szymkiewicz (1912)

Love, sickness, and loneliness in wartime

André Maurois is the artistic pseudonym of Emile Herzog, a French novelist, biographer, essayist, and literary critic. He initiated his career as a writer in the midst of a war, without letting himself be conditioned by that terrible and sorrowful experience. His biographies often referred to the people he admired. In them, the reader progresses through each story without noticing that time is going by, as in real life. One notices a rigorous study of the data, but nicely done, without any pedantry. To this he added an extraordinary psychological and moral interpretation of each person.

André was born in Elbeuf, Rouen, France, on July 26, 1885. He came from a rich Alsatian Jewish family who had moved to Normandy in 1871 and were the owners of a textile factory. In his memoirs he notes that he had a happy childhood that marked his whole life, to which his parents contributed a great deal. Toward them he always showed great admiration.

He was in love with his wife, Jeanne-Marie Wanda de Szymkiewicz, who he married in 1912. He portrays her and their three children with great affection in his memoirs. After Jeanne-Marie died in 1924, André married Simone de Caillevet, a niece of Marcel Proust, and the inspiration of one of the author's personalities in the book *In Search of Lost Time.*

During the First World War he served as an interpreter and liaison officer with the British army and thus familiarized himself with Anglo-Saxon culture. This experience greatly influenced his work. His vocation as a novelist began with his book *Climates* in 1928. In 1938 he entered the Académie Français.

In the Second World War, he served as a captain in the French army. After refusing obedience to the pro-Nazi Vichy government, he took refuge in the United States where he spent a long exile. He died in Paris at the age of eighty-two on October 9, 1967.

The numerous biographies he wrote include those of Shelley, Disraeli, Don Juan, Byron, Chateaubriand, Balzac, Napoleon, and Marcel Proust. Among his novels are *Climates*, in which he recreates his family life, *The Weigher of Souls*, *A Machine for Reading Thoughts*, and *Roses of September*. Especially noteworthy among his essays are *The Art of Living, Literary Studies, The Three Dumas, History of England,* and *History of France.* He wrote *The Professor of Marriage* for the theater. The protagonist is a teacher who gives comical lessons on the art of good marriage and advice on how to increase marital harmony.

A Great Reader Since Childhood

As a child André had at his disposal a well-chosen family library. His mother, very well educated, taught him to read at the age of four and instilled in him a love of reading. In the Lycée of Elbeuf, which he entered at the age of eight, a love of reading was also fostered. To André there remained a thankful memory of those teachers who felt enthusiasm for their work, especially Monsieur Kittel:

> Kittel was the first to tell me that perhaps, with time, I would write books. . . . He gave me a book, *The Russian Soul*, which contained short novels by Pushkin, Gogol, and Tolstoy, on the first page he had written a dedication in which he asked me not to forget him when I had become a writer.
>
> I have never forgotten him. In that book that he gave me I read for the first time *La Dame de Pique*, a story that vividly impressed me and inspired a desire to some day compose fantastic stories like that.[1]

At twelve he began his secondary studies in Rouen, in the Lycée Corneille, from 1897 to 1902. At that age he had already read a great number of books. His teacher, Alain, who opened the path to literature for him, had a great influence on his life:

> The first class with Alain he went to the blackboard and wrote: "It is necessary to seek the truth with all one's soul." He let us think for a few minutes about this phrase of Plato. Alain thought that the best way of forcing people to exercise their judgment was not to offer them already known doctrines, but to stimulate their appetite and their curiosity with continual surprises. . . . I have known few lecturers better than Alain. He entertained with the details of the texts and savored their beauties.[2]

---

1. André Maurois, *Memorias* (Barcelona: Ayma, 1944), 43.
2. Maurois, 61–62.

He graduated with a degree in literature from the University of Caen in 1903 with excellent marks.

Working in a Factory

After his graduation young André considered what he should dedicate himself to. He would have liked to be an honorable professor, loved by his students, who would spend part of his time writing. But Alain as well as his father advised him to work first in the family factory in order to get some life experience before writing—something that did not please him at all:

> Don't seduce me. What should I, a reader of Plato and Descartes, do, among mountains of fabric, between greasy machines and soaked wool? Why should I accept a hard life, almost without vacations, far from my beloved books, when nothing prevents me from living the life for which I feel I was born?[3]

From 1904 until the outbreak of the First World War, he worked in the family textile factory, and then he succeeded in dedicating himself to literature.

Love at First Sight

Young André considered women to be servants and simple instruments of pleasure. But that attitude changed radically when he fell in love with a fascinating woman. A friend who was an actress introduced him, while on vacation in Geneva, to Mademoiselle Jeanne-Marie de Szymkiewicz.

---

3. Maurois, 69.

Disconcerted by the surprising beauty of the young lady, I
did not know what to say. . . . The face of my dreams had
appeared before me. . . . I could not take my eyes from
the apparition which suddenly had filled all the desires of
my heart. She looked at me also and, embarrassed by my
silence, smiled.

"May I accompany you across the park?"

"As you like."

"It's strange," I told her, "but I've been waiting for you
for twenty years."

"I have to return," she said. "The lions will get angry."

"Who are the lions?"

"My mother and my grandmother."

"Can I see you tomorrow?"

"Yes, come to the park at four. Near our bench. I will
be there. We can go and have tea together."[4]

This first meeting with Jeanne-Marie left André with a
memory he could never erase as the years went by.

When I recall that evening, my feelings are a mixture of
admiration, of enthusiasm, and of confidence. From our
first words, our conversation was on a plane of familiarity,
of tenderness, and undoubtedly one must add, of love. I
immediately loved her precise voice, a little bit veiled, and
the sad poetry of her answers. What did she say? She told
me her life.[5]

Jeanne-Marie told him that her mother had been wid-
owed at a very young age with a daughter, Jeanne-Marie herself, whom she placed in a convent, and a son, whom she had

4. Maurois, 121.

5. Maurois, 122.

sent to a boarding school. Since then, she told him, she had felt unhappy; life at home had become unbearable to her.

Courtship

When his vacation ended, André left Jeanne-Marie in Geneva to return to Elbeuf. He then developed the custom of spending every Sunday in Geneva. Every day at eight in the morning, Jeanne-Marie went to wait for him at the station of Cornavin:

> Since she was very religious and did not want to miss Mass, she brought me with her. She was astonished and disconcerted to know that I was not a Catholic. "I will convert you," she told me.
>
> Finding myself at her side in a church, I experienced an infinite sweetness. The music and the Latin of the liturgy were sublime; the Gospel of the day, every Sunday was perfect and mysteriously agreed with our thoughts. Janine had said to me one day at the beginning of our friendship:
>
> "Promise me that you will never try to make me lose my faith . . ."
>
> "My dear," I answered her, "I will try more than anything, if you didn't have it, I would give it to you."[6]

André wanted very much to get married, but he had to wait until she turned twenty and he had a more established position. In addition he had to convince his parents to accept an "exotic" marriage with a Russian. Janine had to do the same with her mother and guardian uncle.

---

6. Maurois, 128.

The Wedding and First Years of Married Life

Finally they were able to fulfill their desire:

> The wedding was celebrated in Paris, on October 30, 1912, in Trinity Church. An old and pleasant priest united us. Taking the hand of Jeanne-Marie in mine, to place the ring on her finger, was very sweet for me. "For better or for worse," she said to me gravely, going down the steps of the Church.[7]

In this new period André felt happier than Jeanne-Marie did. It was a very difficult time for the new wife, for she had to spend many hours alone in a small village with André's family, with whom she did not fit in:

> Our house of Caudebec was simple, but gracious. The good taste of Jeanne-Marie had worked wonders. . . . We had many common tastes and the evenings that we spent together, I reading novels or comedies to her aloud, she playing the piano or telling me about her childhood, were always very agreeable. I desired nothing more. I thought, with a foolish egoism, that she was fully satisfied. I learned a long time after her death, through some letters of hers found by me and by confidences of her friends, that she had experienced an extraordinary pain in acclimating herself in the bosom of an austere and melancholy family. "Our life as hermits," she said. . . . For her those hours of intimacy were separated by the vast deserts of the day.[8]

The only thing that concerned and saddened André was the frustration of not cultivating his literary vocation. On May 27, 1914, Michelle, their first child, was born.

---

7. Maurois, 135.
8. Maurois, 137–138.

Jeanne-Marie was very sick for a long time as a consequence of the birth. André was already close to taking part in the World War with the French army, where he would be an interpreter—and later a liaison officer attached to the general staff of a British army on the Somme River. That, along with his good knowledge of English, made him familiar with the Anglo-Saxon culture and character and later allowed him to write about various aspects of English culture.

Saying Good-Bye to Jeanne-Marie

A separation motivated by a war is one of the most sorrowful there can be between spouses, above all because of the uncertainty about the future. In this case it was harder for Jeanne-Marie, who knew that she would be condemned to a life of loneliness. During their farewell she confessed to him her fear:

> Jeanne-Marie and I spent a sweet and melancholy evening. It was a warm and clear day and we were sitting in the garden, under the trees. We were holding hands and scarcely speaking.
>
> "I hope," I said, "that you have not felt too unhappy, have you?"
>
> "I have been so happy," she said, "that I would like my whole life to be like this past year. . . . But I am afraid of what is coming. . . ."
>
> "My family will take care of you. I have asked them solemnly."
>
> "Yes," she replied, "they will try to, but they don't know how to. . . . With you gone, there is no longer any bond between us."[9]

---

9. Maurois, 145.

A friend offered himself to drive André to the camp in Rouen. Before parting, Jeanne-Marie, accompanied by her daughter, embraced him. A compassionate English captain freed him from going to the front, instead giving him the job of organizing provisions.

> "But captain," I replied, "I prefer to go with the others. I want to take part in the war."
>
> "You will have plenty of time for that," said Ridel. "It will be a long one. You must think of your hapless wife. She has told my wife about her situation. She has no family in this country. She has not yet gotten used to yours and has not yet recovered from the nervous shock of giving birth. She has hidden her state from you, but she is desperate."[10]

André and Jeanne-Marie's Meetings During the War

André thought of different means of seeing his wife during the war. But at that time he was not conscious of the enormous sacrifice those sporadic meetings caused her.

> She frequently reproached me later for my blindness during this time. Men never understand the tremendous fatigues of their wives. The one that I adored suffered from a nervous exhaustion which put her in danger, and I did not see anything. I made her travel for days for the pleasure of seeing her for an hour. I did not think of organizing life for her happiness, but rather made her life compatible with my duties as a soldier.[11]

---

10. Maurois, 152.
11. Maurois, 152.

Finding himself in the French military hospital of Le Havre, a doctor who was a friend of his put him under observation for three months, and André went to live at the base:

> Having some time at my disposal, I acquired a rather agreeable house at the foot of the Sainte-Adresse Hill, and had my wife and daughter come. This was prohibited since Le Havre was in a battle zone, but all of my superiors, converted into friends, closed their eyes. Seeing my daughter was a big surprise. At that age they change rapidly. Michelle now could talk and run. Her mother was proud of her. In that little garden in Le Havre we experienced hours that recalled the sweetness of the past. . . . Jeanne-Marie was happy. She had found some friends in Le Havre. But in time of war nothing lasts long.[12]

Jeanne-Marie's Loneliness Causes a Marital Crisis

André was right in saying that, in time of war, nothing is lasting. Because of her loneliness, Jeanne-Marie distanced herself from her husband, which led to a marital crisis:

> I had the right to a furlough every four months. The first time I went to Paris, to our little apartment on the Rue Ampère. She was restless due to an indefinable and painful feeling of discomfort. As could easily be foreseen, Jeanne-Marie, alone in Paris, and being so beautiful, had little by little been found by different groups whose life was not the studious, quiet and modest one that I had wished for her. I was far away, and knowing that I would not like some of those new friends, she did not speak of

---

12. Maurois, 164–165.

them in her letters. . . . During the whole of this leave she made a gentle and careful effort to make me happy. But I wasn't and I left her carrying with me the memory of mysterious phone calls and incomprehensible allusions. She realized this and on the platform of the North Station she embraced me with an anxious and desperate tenderness. . . . Her life and mine, outside of our daughter and our memories had little in common. The war was undoing our marriage, as it had so many others.[13]

André recognized, many years later, that during that period his love for Jeanne-Marie was more proper to the courtship stage, when one usually idealizes the person loved:

In that time I wrote many letters to my wife in verse, but they were directed to the Natasha, to the Irene of my imagination, more than to the real and helpless woman who needed a presence, a support, and not just poetic declarations.[14]

André Publishes His First book

The experience of the war influenced his literary beginnings in a decisive way. In 1918, although still mobilized, he published the book *The Silence of Colonel Bramble,* under the pseudonym of "André Maurois." It was a humorous tale of his experiences in the war. The good reception of this work led him to write the following:

The end of the year 1917 was for me, as for everyone, unhappy. The war seemed interminable and victory

13. Maurois, 169.
14. Maurois, 169.

uncertain. A shadow overcast my personal life. I sought refuge in fiction. For some time a great number of people were being nourished in my dreams. They were born as much from myself as from the officers that I had met in the Ninth Division, or from my friends and comrades of the Asser General Staff. . . . During the nights at Abbeville, awaiting the growling of the German airplanes, and in order to flee from my dark thoughts, I set myself to noting down the dialogues of these men. Soon, these conversations took the form of a book. I wrote it on the typewriter of the General Staff in my moments of relaxation. Later I came up with a title: *The Silence of Colonel Bramble.*[15]

Jeanne-Marie Becomes Gravely Ill

The Allied armies began to win the war, but André could not savor this success because of a new and grave infirmity of his wife, of which he had been informed by a telegram from a doctor. After getting a military leave for a few days, he went to visit her and brought her to a hospital in Paris, where he had to leave her. It hurt him to return to the war when his wife needed him the most. Jeanne-Marie's sickness and its effects on their marital life created great anxiety in André. Therefore the imminent military victory was for him a mere routine. He felt very pessimistic in regard to his marriage:

My marriage? Even if Jeanne-Marie is cured, she will feel cruelly dealt with by my absence, by the hostile influences, by her fate. . . . Undoubtedly I have a new happiness now: that of writing. But, what does success mean, even when I enjoy my work, if no one can participate in it? My

---

15. Maurois, p.170.

wife seemed indifferent to this new aspect of my life. My friends, those I loved most had died. My daughter, the only hope of the future, was four years old. Of the edifice patiently constructed during the first part of my life, almost nothing remains. In that night of victory, when I found myself alone in my room, I felt exhausted, beaten.[16]

André was demobilized at the beginning of 1919. He was thirty-three years old. At that point he decided to make a 180-degree turn in his life: "I came up with a plan, inconceivable four years earlier, of abandoning my factory, my city and my province, and going to rebuild somewhere else, according to a new plan, a life which the war had left in ruins." [17]

The Return to Elbeuf

André tried to think how he could help Jeanne-Marie recover her health. For this he followed the doctors' advice:

The doctors, for the convalescence of my wife had advised me to live outside of the town, and I had rented a very nice house surrounded by a small park in the nearby village of Elbeuf. . . . Did Jeanne-Marie become accustomed to the new house? I don't think so. She had returned from that other war, sickness, with a withered body and soul. . . . To her melancholy nature there was mixed a singular bitterness. Abandoned, without a protector, without counsel, in a world that the disorder of the time had made implacable and dangerous, she had encountered treachery, perfidy, and cruelty.[18]

16. Maurois, 175–176.

17. Maurois, 175–177.

18. Maurois, 182.

André did not have success in bringing about Jeanne-Marie's recovery, for he was not capable of seeing and accepting her as she was in their new personal situation. His help was more of a material than a spiritual type. He also recognized that he had been egoistic in regard to his wife. He thought more of his own happiness than of hers:

> To reconquer Janine I was disposed to make all kinds of sacrifices, but not the intellectual sacrifice that would have consisted, I repeat, in accepting her as she was. The pleasures of the artist, that I had begun to savor, attracted me more than those of love. The egoism of the writer, with more devotion to his work than to the beings that surrounded him, a strange combination of maternal solicitude and of paternal ambition, grew openly in me. Our marriage, apparently tranquil beneath the beautiful linden trees of La Saussaye, suffered.[19]

In these difficult circumstances, André saw himself reflected in the poet Shelley, which led him to write his biography, *Ariel: The Life of Shelley.*

> Since my first visits to Oxford I had pondered with vivid interest the life of the poet Shelley, and it seemed to me that in writing about him, I could express the feelings that I had experienced and that still bothered me. Like Shelley, converted under the influence of my juvenile readings into a doctrinaire, I had tried to apply rational methods to my emotional life. Like him, I had encountered a living and sensitive matter that did not give way to my logic. Like him, I had suffered and made others suffer.[20]

---

19. Maurois, 182.
20. Maurois, 182–183.

The book's publication in 1923 was a great success.

Jeanne-Marie Reads *Ariel: The Life of Shelley*

Reading André's book, Jeanne-Marie learned to appreciate its author, but it also served to denounce the inconsistencies of her husband:

> *Ariel* had in Jeanne-Marie an attentive, concerned, and surprised reader. Until that book, my wife had not given great importance to my vocation as a writer. . . . She now had three children (the latest ones, Gerald and Olivier, had been born in 1920 and 1921) and did not have any wish to see me abandon a prosperous factory, for work of doubtful success. . . . After *Ariel*, she was more indulgent and respectful in regard to my work.
>
> "I did not think you were capable of writing this book," she told me, ". . . You speak here about women better than you ever spoke to me . . ."
>
> "Who knows," I answered her, "if I wrote this precisely to tell you things that I could not bring myself to tell you out loud."
>
> She had read the manuscript. She reread the printed book twice. She sought in it allusions, explanations. She copied passages. I understood that she was surprised to see that I seemed to reproach Shelley for precisely what she suffered from me, that inflexible seriousness that she called "my pedantry," that need to surround myself with professors that she considered unbearably annoying, and that unconscious and hard egoism of the artist. Since he understands so well, she seemed to think, why doesn't he change?[21]

---

21. Maurois, 201–202.

The Marital Crisis Continues

André and Jeanne-Marie entered into an epoch of separate lives that saddened them, but which they were not able to correct. Their sole point of support was the good memories they shared:

> I then had some friends in Paris, to whose homes I went to spend the evening without her. For her part, Jeanne-Marie frequently went out with her brother, who had become a great fashion designer in a world unknown to me. Both of us looked on with desperation as the rift caused by four years of war increased between us. Like a man with his feet sunk into the mire, moves in vain and sinks deeper, our efforts to be loving, our small sacrifices, went unnoticed, misunderstood, and poorly repaid, making us clearly feel the danger of our situation. . . . And since the love between Jeanne-Marie and myself had so many happy memories, as our love had begun with so much strength and confidence, we could not consent to a spiritual divorce.[22]

During this period of sickness and marital crisis, Jeanne-Marie struggled to save her marriage and her family:

> For Christmas Jeanne-Marie had a mind to prepare gifts and a tree. She very much liked feasts and presents. She sent to London, secretly for me, the sixty volumes of the Dictionary of National Biography, whose absence in our library she had heard me lament so many times. I can still see her joy on the day that she led me to the shelves on which the surprise had been placed.[23]

---

22. Maurois, 203.
23. Maurois, 203–204.

Corresponding to Jeanne-Marie's positive attitude, André sacrificed himself more than ever before for his wife and his children:

> Even though it was not the time of vacation, and in spite of the complaints of my associates, I abandoned the factory in full operation and moved with my wife and the children to La Napoule, near Cannes. Jeanne-Marie had a group of English and American friends there whom we both loved. We hardly left the house and the beach. We had long and frank conversations.[24]

Jeanne-Marie's Death

This period of peace and togetherness was interrupted once more by Jeanne-Marie's health. A violent fever forced her to stay in bed. The doctors diagnosed a severe infection and decided to operate:

> Jeanne-Marie accepted the operation with courage, but without illusions. She asked to see the children again. . . . When the chloroform wore off and she woke up, she suffered a lot. I was at her side with a nurse. Jeanne-Marie spoke as someone who was going to die and knew it. She said that she was a believer and asked me to have Masses said for the repose of her soul. Suddenly, she launched a cry of terror: "I can't see!" Her head fell on the pillow. All had ended. I could not believe it nor admit it . . . Until morning I knelt close to the small bed, holding that hand as it grew cold. . . . I went out in search of flowers. I returned with my arms full of lilies and roses, which I placed next to

---

24. Maurois, 205.

her. . . . In the enormous world I had encountered the queen. I had chosen her, won her and lost her. . . . In the morning the first friends came. . . . In the Church of Saint-Pierre of Neuilly I had them play the Requiem of Fauré, which is so beautiful, and Handel's Largo.[25]

The experience that André had at Jeanne-Marie's funeral produced an effect similar to a religious conversion in him:

For the touching beauty of this Mass, I owe the Church an infinite thanks. I was consumed by sorrow and love. . . . It seemed possible to be peaceful, and if there exists another world where the one I loved so much was still living, I would be there. She would be happy and seem entirely to be the young angel, childlike and passionate that I had seen that first night, by the light of the moon, beneath the trees of the Eaux-Vives Park.[26]

The loss of a spouse is always a deep wound. André explained seventeen years afterward how sorrowful it was for him:

What is most sorrowful after the death of a loved one, for those who remain, is the feeling that it is irreparable: Never more. Never more will I hear that somewhat veiled voice. Never more will I see her beautiful face. Never more will I be able to have with her that which she called "a word." A long explanation focused at times on a difficult point, but which now seems to me so precious that I would gladly give what remains of my life to see Janine again for an hour, for a minute.[27]

25. Maurois, 206.
26. Maurois, 205–206.
27. Maurois, 209.

The great emotional impact of losing his wife prevented him from working. The permanent memory of Jeanne-Marie left no space for anything else:

> Every night, in my dreams I meet Jeanne-Marie again. Every time I wake up it is like a tearing apart. . . . Before the grave I placed a small semi-circular marble bench, a willow tree, and a large vase of flowers. I became used to going each day to sit in that cemetery to dream of the past. Frequently the children accompanied me. . . . As soon as I had the heart for it, I went back to work.[28]

▪ ▪ ▪

They Married Very Much in Love

For young André it was providential to meet Jeanne-Marie. He admired both her personal qualities and her consistency with her beliefs, which led him to fall in love with her, and be transformed by her, beginning with his view of women, which he no longer saw as instruments of pleasure. Jeanne-Marie's impact can be seen by the fact that he converted to Catholicism during their courtship and wanted to be married soon in the Church. In the story of their marriage one has to first give "credit" to André—his love was authentic, beautiful, and romantic.

His first meeting with Jeanne-Marie left André with a memory that he could never erase. In the years that followed there was a greater appreciation of Jeanne-Marie's personal qualities. Out of this grew admiration. He was in love with her personhood, her spirituality, not only her physical beauty. And in that love there were noble sentiments: enthusiasm, confidence, and tenderness. The relationship between them

---

28. Maurois, 209–211.

was characterized by personal contact, through very open conversations full of trust and respect. Each told the other of their earlier life, facilitating their mutual desire to know each other. André married very much in love and was a good newly married husband.

Jeanne-Marie's Loneliness Provokes a Marital Crisis

André did not realize how much Jeanne-Marie suffered, without complaining, from being alone in a house in an isolated village, living with her in-laws, with whom she did not get along. The only thing that bothered him was not being able to cultivate his literary vocation. Later there was added loneliness because of the war. Although he succeeded in reuniting with her, he did it without being conscious of the sacrifice those sporadic meetings caused her; she carried on without complaining, "for better or for worse."

Contrary to what André supposed, the cause of the couple's marital crisis was not the war but his own blindness. Undoubtedly, he loved his wife a lot, but he did not always make her a priority. Even after she was seriously ill, there was a moment when he put his literary vocation ahead of her. The dialogue between the couple after Jeanne-Marie's reading of *Ariel* is very significant. For the first time she reproached him for his inconsistencies in love.

It is surprising that an author who wrote so well about love should have made the mistakes of a beginner. Let us look at one of his rules regarding the art of loving included in his book *The Art of Living:*

> To nurture a love requires constant care. The most powerful of attractions, the courtship, is also the most perishable.

At the beginning of a love, each person has a thousand things to discover in the other. But these reserves are used up, and quite soon the stories that appeared so new become monotonous, worn out. The genius in love consists in preserving in the union a perpetual newness.[29]

A woman like Jeanne-Marie, who knew how to love her husband and always tried to save her marriage even when she was ill, received love, but she deserved something more. She deserved to be first in her husband's life.

Many crises result from the fact that one spouse puts his or her professional work in first place. For a married person, the first priority is never one's work—it's one's spouse and children. It's true that it is sometimes hard to harmonize family and work, but one has to treat it as a challenge to one's ingeniousness and creativity. Almost always the cord is broken at its weakest point—the family—and this shows an incorrect hierarchy of values. A spouse deserves preferential attention on the part of the other spouse.

Jeanne-Marie deserved greater trust and openness from her husband, and she did not expect to have to get to know him by reading one of his books. He could have made use of letters, which was very appropriate in time of war. Jeanne-Marie needed the constant care that her husband explained in his books. André gave her material help and a comfortable house but little spiritual assistance. He loved her, but not as she needed to be loved.

He did not understand his wife's feelings in her new and difficult circumstances, probably because he no longer sought to get to know his beloved as he had done during

---

29. André Maurois, *Un Arte de Vivir* (Buenos Aires: Libreria Hachette, 1955), chapter 2.

their engagement and the beginning of their marriage. He did not experience married love as the perpetual newness he wrote about in his books. Such a failure is worrisome, not only because it denotes egocentrism and routine, but also because it is a kind of infidelity.

> Love is a continual discovery and appreciation of the other as other. This discovery is an unending process that gradually spreads itself out throughout a lifetime. In this sense, the virtue of fidelity does not mean simply avoiding infidelity, but an opening to the reality of the other, a reality that one cannot know in advance. Fidelity is the desire to accept the other person as he or she is presented to us. Fidelity is not static. It takes it for granted that the two people are in a state of constant change, discovering who they really are, but always with an attitude of fidelity toward the changes of the other. The "us" that emerges from this situation transcends the particular being of each one.[31]

We know the marital crisis was overcome by Jeanne-Marie's efforts to save her marriage and her family. This included paying detailed attention to her husband. Her behavior stimulated André's reaction, and he began to put his family ahead of his work. André's sorrow during Jeanne-Marie's illness and death showed that, as a husband, he had come out of the crisis strengthened.

Crises in married love are not signs of failure; they are opportunities to renew a couple's love—they are invitations to love more and to love better.

---

31. Robert Constable, "Educación Familiar y Terapia Familiar: Guía para el Cambio en Las Relaciones." Speech given at the Second Interfamily Conference at the University of Navarra, October of 2003.

Chapter 15

J.R.R. TOLKIEN AND EDITH BRATT (1916)

Love for their children helped them stay united to the end

John Ronald Reuel Tolkien was born on January 3, 1892, in Bloemfontein, South Africa. His father, Arthur Reuel Tolkien, was an English banker who emigrated from Birmingham to South Africa (at that time a British Colony) in search of better opportunities. There he married Mabel Suffield, of English origin, who was thirteen years younger. The wedding ceremony was celebrated in the cathedral of Capetown on April 6, 1891. Mabel accepted the sacrifice of living five thousand miles from her home in Birmingham in a land unknown to her. She did this out of love for her husband.

> She adored Arthur, and she was happy when she could entice him from his desk and they could go for walks or drives, play a game of tennis or a round of golf, or read aloud to each other. Soon there was something else to occupy her mind: the realisation that she was pregnant.[1]

---

1. Humphrey Carpenter, *J.R.R. Tolkien: A Biography* (New York: Houghton Mifflin, 2000), 20.

Their first son, John Ronald Reuel, was baptized in the cathedral of Bloemfontein on January 31, 1892. On February 17, 1894, a second son, Hilary Arthur Reuel, was born. The extremely hot climate of Bloemfontein seemed to negatively affect the health of the children, and therefore Mabel, with her husband's agreement, moved to Birmingham temporarily with the intention of eventually returning to South Africa.

Arthur remained alone in South Africa. In 1896 he contracted rheumatic fever. Mabel decided to return to take care of him, but she did not arrive in time. He died on February 15 of that year and was buried in the Anglican cemetery of Bloemfontein. The income remaining for Mabel was barely enough to maintain her and her two children. Therefore she had to rent a small house in Sarehole, a small rural community on the outskirts of Birmingham. In that world of meadows, forests, and rivers, the fantasy of John Ronald was awakened. The recollection of that happy childhood in the open air was a constant factor in his creative works. Mabel worked hard to maintain her family and was concerned with the religious education of her children.

A Young Widow and Mother Converts to Catholicism

Mabel initially raised her children according to her Anglican religion, but after being received into the Catholic Church in 1900, along with her sister May, she gave them a Catholic education. Her conversion alienated her from some of her family members who deprived her of financial support. But her faith prevailed during a period when converting to Catholicism in England was looked upon as high treason.

Mabel was careful to make sure that her two sons were good students so they could obtain scholarships to a private school. John Ronald remained a Catholic all his life, edified by the example of courage and consistency of his mother:

> My own dear mother was a martyr indeed, and it is not everybody that God grants so easy a way to his great gifts as he did to Hilary and myself, giving us a mother who killed herself with labour and trouble to ensure us keeping the faith.[2]

Thanks to his mother, John Ronald learned to read at the age of four. At the age of seven he knew Latin, Greek, French, and German. Mabel also read him many storybooks, although he preferred the legends of dragons to classic stories. They moved to Birmingham in 1900, where John began his studies in King Edward's School, the school his father had attended. From an early age he showed an interest in language and cultivated a hobby of inventing languages. He also demonstrated an extraordinary linguistic capacity in both classic and modern languages.

In 1902, with his brother Hilary, John Ronald entered St. Philip's Grammar School. The new family home was very close to the Oratory of Birmingham, which had been founded in 1849 by John Henry Newman after his conversion from Anglicanism to Catholicism. One of the priests of that community, Fr. Francis Morgan, had taken charge of the parish. He was a valuable friend of the Tolkien family. Two years later Mabel became sick with diabetes, which was incurable in those days when insulin was not yet known. After spending some weeks in a hospital, she

---

2. Carpenter, 31.

entered a diabetic coma and died in November 1902 at the age of thirty-four.

Two Orphaned Boys

The boys at this time were twelve and eleven years old. John Ronald was very much affected by his mother's death and fell into frequent states of pessimism and depression. The loss of his mother stayed with him all his life, although he was sustained by his faith and also found a wonderful refuge in books. His main interest was books that contained legends and mythologies. He also took refuge in Scripture and in nature. He was attracted especially by the beauty of trees; he liked to be near them, observe them, climb them, and sketch them.

The two orphans had been entrusted by their mother to Fr. Morgan's tutelage—he took charge of them materially and spiritually, becoming their tutor and mentor. He installed them in the home of their aunt, Beatrice Suffield. This woman limited herself to providing lodging and food: her lack of affection made her nephews unhappy. For that reason, in 1908 Fr. Morgan decided to seek a better place for them. He found a Mrs. Faulkner, who ran a kind of boardinghouse. Once accepted there, the Tolkien brothers got to know another boarder, a girl of nineteen who worked many hours each day at her sewing machine. Her name was Edith Bratt, and she too was an orphan.

Edith had been born on January 21, 1889, in Gloucester. She was illegitimate—her mother, Frances Bratt, never married. The girl had musical talent and played the piano well. After her mother died she studied music at school, hoping to become a piano teacher and concert pianist. Her musical career was interrupted when her guardian sent her to the boardinghouse.

A Storybook Courtship

Edith and John liked each other from the beginning. Together they began to frequent the teahouses of Birmingham and take bicycle rides together. Between the two orphans, both in need of affection, there soon arose a secret romance in the summer of 1909. Fr. Morgan discovered the romance upon noticing that John's marks had started to decline. He became upset, feeling himself deceived by a person to whom he had given so much affection and help. He also worried because John was becoming careless in his studies just before the examination that could lead to the scholarship he needed to get into Oxford. The boy failed his exams that year and did not obtain it.

Fr. Morgan demanded that John Ronald cut off his relationship with Edith. He wanted to prevent the boy's intellectual gifts from being lost because of an immature love. Another factor was that the lovers were of different religions. Edith was a Protestant. Morgan ordered John to move out of the boardinghouse where Edith was living. After their separation the lovers sent notes by means of messengers, but Morgan prohibited this also. He told John Ronald that he could not see her until he was "of age" (twenty-one). The youth obeyed because he owed every-thing to Fr. Morgan and because he believed that author-ity existed to be obeyed. But he kept his feelings alive, as did Edith:

> Father Francis was not a clever man, and he did not per-ceive that by compelling Ronald and Edith to part he was transforming a boy-and-girl love-affair into a thwarted romance. Ronald himself wrote thirty years later: "Probably nothing else would have strengthened our will to the point

of giving permanence to the relationship—although it was, undoubtedly, a case of true love . . ."[3]

The period of waiting was for Tolkien a trial of love, during which he demonstrated sacrifice and fidelity to the woman he loved. He had discovered those values in the Christianity he had learned from his mother and also from his readings of medieval literature, where women were highly honored.

Edith abandoned Duchess Road to move to Cheltenham, taking up residence in the house of a couple that had always offered her their protection even though they were not related. The young woman found a home there along with a peace that was new for her. She could practice the piano every day and played at the services of the parish church.

In 1910 Tolkien won the Exhibition Scholarship for Exeter College of Oxford. The following year he began his studies for a bachelor's degree in English at Oxford, which he completed in 1915 with first-class honors. In January 1913 he began teaching in the Honors School of English Language and Literature. That same month he also attained his long-awaited twenty-first birthday.

> On the stroke of midnight, at the very beginning of 3 January 1913, Tolkien celebrated his coming of age by sitting up in bed and writing his first letter to her for almost three years. It was a renewal of his declaration of love, which culminated in the question which was uppermost in his mind: "How long will it be before we can be joined together before God and the world?"[4]

---

3. Carpenter, 52.

4. Joseph Pearce, *Tolkien: Man and Myth, A Literary Life* (San Francisco: Ignatius, 2001) 33.

Edith answered that she was already committed to another young man—she thought John Ronald had forgotten her. Tolkien did not give up; he took the first train to Cheltenham. At the station Edith was waiting for him. After walking and talking for several hours, Edith agreed to marry him. It was not difficult, since she had never stopped loving him, and therefore the relationship continued where it had left off.

Tolkien returned to Oxford and announced to Fr. Morgan his plans to marry Edith. The response was cold, due to the fact that she was an Anglican and was living in the house of an anti-Catholic Protestant. But Tolkien remained calm. He was confident that his fiancée would enter the Catholic Church; although currently she had very different beliefs and customs, he didn't believe that would prevent them from eventually marrying. John Ronald's optimism was unrealistic, since although Edith was agreeable to the idea of converting to Catholicism, actually doing so was full of obstacles. She feared being persecuted and ostracized. She would have to give up her numerous friends in the Anglican Church while continuing to live in the house of someone who was anti-Catholic.

On January 8, 1914, Edith entered the Catholic Church at the insistence of her fiancé, although she still had some hesitation. For this reason she harbored a certain resentment. Shortly thereafter they committed themselves before Fr. Murphy. That day Edith went to confession and received Communion for the first time, which gave her great joy.

John Ronald and Edith's Wedding

In order to marry, Edith gave up all her personal ambitions; she sacrificed much to be Tolkien's wife, and she continued to do so throughout her life. In 1915 Tolkien enlisted for combat in the First World War. As the moment approached to embark for France to join his combat unit, the two young people decided to marry before he left, in spite of not having any income other than his very small army pay. He was twenty-four and she was twenty-seven.

On March 22, 1916, they were married at St. Mary Immaculate Church in Warwick. The ceremony was officiated by Fr. Murphy. The beauty of the place, set in the countryside, was an ideal setting for a romantic union such as theirs.

Tolkien served as battalion signal officer at the Somme front. He saw to it that the tragedy of war did not change his way of contemplating the world, his enthusiasm for life, and his faith. During this period he wrote a poem, which was a canticle to love:

> Lo! Young we are and yet have stood
> like planted hearts in the great Sun
> of Love so long (as two fair trees
> in woodland or in open dale
>
> stand utterly entwined, and breathe
> the airs, and suck the very light
>
> together), that we have become
> as one, deep-rooted in the soil
> of Life, and tangled in the sweet growth.

In November Tolkien returned to England, sick with trench fever, a bacterial infection spread by lice that abounded in the trenches, and complicated by trench foot, a painful foot ailment similar to frostbite. Edith devoted herself to caring for him. She was a good nurse who brought him back to health. He never forgot the happiness she gave him, especially during the long walks through a grove of hemlocks.

J.R.R. Tolkien and Edith Bratt (1916) ▪ 241

Edith sang and danced for him among the trees. In 1917, still convalescing, he began to write *The Book of the Lost Tales*, which later became *The Silmarillion*. It depicted the history of love between a mortal man, Beren, and an immortal maiden, Luthien. His love for Edith deepened upon seeing her playing in the forest.

That year Tolkien's son John was born. A year later, after the armistice, he returned to Oxford with his family and joined the team working on the *New English Dictionary*. In 1920 he was appointed "reader" of English at the University of Leeds, and his second son Michael, was born. In 1924 he was appointed professor of English at Leeds, and his third son, Christopher, arrived. A year later he became the Rawlinson and Bosworth professor of Anglo-Saxon at Oxford and acquired a house on Northmoor Road. His family was reunited with him shortly afterward. In 1929 their first and only daughter, Priscilla, was born.

Oxford Is Difficult for Edith

When Tolkien became a professor at Oxford, Edith had a difficult time. She missed her life in Leeds, where the people were simpler. She felt uncomfortable among the other professors' wives who were more highly educated than she was. For this reason she did not take the initiative in organizing social gatherings. She became known as "the wife who does not call," and was excluded from the social gatherings organized by the other wives in their homes. Edith was also not happy with the excessive dedication of her husband to his many great friends, especially to C.S. Lewis, which made her feel ignored.

Another issue was that Tolkien was excessively dedicated to his work and found interruptions annoying when he was writing. Nevertheless he counted on her to read what he was writing and make copies. Fortunately they did have a few friends in common. In 1945 Tolkien was appointed professor of English Language and Literature at Merton College of Oxford.

The house on Holywell Street where the Tolkiens lived was disturbed by the noise and exhaust of traffic, making work and sleep difficult. Therefore in 1953 they bought a house on Sanfield Road in Headington, a quiet suburb of Oxford. It had the inconvenience that if one wanted to travel to Headington from the center of the city, one had to take a taxi, which cut down on visits by Tolkien's friends. In 1954 the first volume of *The Lord of the Rings* was published. In 1959 Tolkien retired from his professorship at Oxford.

Tolkien leaves Oxford to Make Edith Happier

In 1968 the Tolkiens moved from Sanfield Road to Bournemouth, an isolated and quiet place on the coast. This was a great sacrifice for John Ronald, for it distanced him even more from Oxford and his intimate friendships. He did it for Edith. He felt that he owed it to her for the many sacrifices she had made:

> But the sacrifice had a purpose to it, and that purpose was achieved. Edith was happy at Lakeside Road, as happy as she had been during the holidays at the Miramar, and consistently happier than she had ever been before in their married life. Besides the comfort of the new house and the benefit she derived from the absence of stairs to be negotiated, there was also her continuing pleasure at visits to the Miramar and at the friendships she made there. She had ceased to be the shy, uncertain, sometimes troubled wife of an Oxford professor, and became herself once more, the sociable good-humoured Miss Bratt of the Cheltenham days. She was back

in the setting where she really belonged. And on the whole life was better for Tolkien himself. Edith's happiness was deeply gratifying to him, and was reflected in his own state of mind, so that the diary he kept for a brief time during these Bournemouth years shows very little of the despondency which often overtook him at Sandfield Road.[5]

In the summer of 1971 Edith suffered an inflammation of the gallbladder that required her to be hospitalized. She died on November 19 of that year at the age of eighty-two, which brought great sadness to Tolkien. Their marriage had lasted fifty-five years. On the day of her death, Tolkien described her last days in a letter to a friend:

> I am grieved to tell you that my wife died this morning. Her courage and determination [. . .] carried her through to what seemed the brink of recovery, but a sudden relapse occurred which she fought for nearly three days in vain. She died at last in peace. I am utterly bereaved, and cannot yet lift up heart, but my family is gathering round me and many friends.[6]

Tolkien was from that moment on a solitary man, but he remained active. In 1972 he returned to Oxford. The university awarded him an honorary doctorate in letters for his work in philology. He took up once again his unfinished novel *The Silmarillion*. It would eventually be published by his son Christopher. On September 2, 1973, Tolkien became sick and died in Bournemouth as a result of stomach complications at the age of eighty-one, two years after his beloved wife, whose loss he had never gotten over. He was buried at her side.

---

5. Carpenter, *J.R.R. Tolkien*, 250.
6. Carpenter, *The Letters of J.R.R. Tolkien* (New York: Houghton Mifflin, 2000), 415.

Edith was the great love of Tolkien's life, and to honor this deep and romantic feeling, Tolkien dedicated to her the sad but beautiful story narrated in *The Silmarillion*. The love between two fictional characters, Luthien and Beren, was based on his own relationship with Edith. Edith and Tolkien were Luthien and Beren until the grave, where the names of both are engraved along with their fictional pseudonyms. The couple's epitaph in the Wolvercote cemetery of Oxford was written by Tolkien a few days before his death and reads thus: "Edith Mary Tolkien, Luthien, 1889–1971; John Ronald Reuel Tolkien, Beren, 1892–1973."

A Romantic Love that Lasted a Lifetime

Tolkien and Edith were friends before falling in love, and they did not cease to be friends in their engagement and throughout their lengthy married life. The spiritual affinity that existed between these true friends helped to ensure that their love was a personal encounter. For the Tolkiens married life was an uninterrupted conversation and a permanent mutual conquest. Their engagement prepared them well for marriage because they knew how to wait; they were persevering in their love. Afterward they loved each other throughout their lives as they did when they were engaged, with the same loving care. There was sacrifice on both parts, each seeking the happiness of the other. Edith sacrificed her religion, her musical career, her world, her time, her relaxation, and her possible fame, for her husband. She was willing to stay in the background in order to support the creative work of the genius she had married. He corresponded in kind, always recognizing his debt of love and making her the protagonist of a great novel of love, which he spent many years writing.

Edith (Luthien): The Protagonist of a Self-Sacrificing and Generous Love

Why did Tolkien want the name "Luthien" to be inscribed on Edith's tombstone? She was the elfin maiden who sacrificed her immortality in order to marry the mortal Beren. In a letter to his son Christopher, he explained it this way:

> She was (and knew she was) my Luthien. . . . Someone close in heart to me should know something about things that records do not record: the dreadful sufferings of our childhoods, from which we rescued one another, but could not wholly heal wounds that later often proved disabling; the sufferings that we endured after our love began—all of which (over and above personal weaknesses) might help to make pardonable, or understandable, the lapses and darknesses which at times marred our lives—and to explain how these never touched our depths nor dimmed the memories of our youthful love. For ever (especially when alone) we still met in the woodland glade and went hand in hand many times to escape the shadow of imminent death before our last parting.[7]

Tolkien and Edith's different ways of being and the different religious educations they had received created a certain psychological distance in the beginning of their married life. Edith, who in the first years after her conversion, showed a lukewarm acceptance of her new creed and was not very devout, did not understand her husband's religious fervor, which she considered exaggerated. Tolkien was always immersed in his world of fiction, while Edith remained in her domestic world:

---

7. Carpenter, *Letters*, 421.

He, who, in his mythological world scarcely touched the ground with his feet, found it difficult to understand how women could lose themselves in the thousand little details of daily life. He found this fastidious and irritating. This was a constant in his married life, which had to be conquered by generosity and good will on his part. He never got used to the triviality that home life brought with it. And she never understood at all the passion of her husband for books and language. They had really been formed in different worlds: a society entirely academic and formal, on one side, and domestic on the other. Worlds that never managed to converge, but which ran parallel throughout their lives. She never managed to participate in the academic and erudite activities of her husband, and he, although he helped her in domestic tasks, always felt that his real place was the public square.[8]

They lived harmoniously together during the fifty-five years they were married because they were able to accept and love each other, seeing a positive complementarity in their differences. Edith was the force that pushed Tolkien to outdo himself in his career and work. They overcame their distance through a proper understanding of married love: a love of self-giving, conceding, and generosity to each other. Persons who knew the two for many years reported that they loved each other very much:

It was visible both in the small things, the almost absurd degree in which each worried about the other's health, and the care in which they chose and wrapped each other's birthday presents; and in the large matters, the way in which

8. Paulino Arguijo, *Tolkien* (Madrid: Palabra, 1992), 78–79.

Ronald willingly abandoned such a large part of his life in retirement to give Edith the last years at Bournemouth that he felt she deserved, and the degree to which she showed pride in his fame as an author. A principal source of happiness to them was their shared love of their family. This bound them together until the end of their lives, and it was perhaps the strongest force in the marriage. They delighted to discuss and mull over every detail of the lives of their children, and later of their grandchildren.[9]

In a letter written in March 1941, Tolkien spoke of the need for sacrifice in one's married life. He was not speaking theoretically but from the shared experience with his wife:

Faithfulness in Christian marriage entails that: great mortification. [. . .] No man, however truly he loved his betrothed and bride as a young man, has lived faithful to her as a wife in mind and body without deliberate conscious exercise of the will, without self-denial.[10]

---

9. Carpenter, *J.R.R. Tolkien*, 161.
10. Carpenter, *Letters*, 51.

Chapter 16

❧

FABIOLA DE MORA
OF ARAGÓN AND BAUDOUIN I
OF BELGIUM (1960)

The happiness of sharing deep religious convictions

King Baudouin I of Belgium was born in Brussels, on September 7, 1930. He was the second son of Leopold III and his first wife, Princess Astrid, granddaughter of King Gustav of Sweden. On August 29, 1935, at the age of five, Baudouin lost his mother due to a traffic accident. In May 1940 the Germans invaded Belgium, and the Belgian army capitulated. A year later Leopold III married Lillian Baels, who later became Princess of Rethy. From June 1944 to July 1945, the Belgian royal family was deported by the Germans, first to Germany and later to Austria. From 1945 to 1950 they lived in exile in Switzerland.

On July 22, 1950, the royal family returned to Belgium. Although the crown was returned to Leopold, he was badly received by the people. On July 16, 1951, Leopold III abdicated and Baudouin I was proclaimed as the fifth king of the Belgians.

Baudouin Becomes King at Age Twenty-One

Baudouin I was sworn in on July 17, 1951. He was a sad king, because he had never wanted to be one and also because of the suffering that accompanied him throughout his life. When he was five his mother died; at ten he became a prisoner of the Germans; at fourteen he was deported; at fifteen he went into exile; at twenty-one he suffered the humiliating abdication of his beloved father, which he considered a grave injustice; and after ascending the throne, he suffered from his stepmother's unwanted political interference. He married when he was thirty, but he failed to have the children he so much wanted.

Baudouin came to the throne in difficult circumstances: He was still very young and had not had enough time to prepare for such a responsibility due to his father's unexpected abdication. His knowledge of his own country was limited by the fact that he had had to live abroad from the ages of ten to twenty. The exhaustion that the exercise of power produced, coupled with his reserved and anxious character, proved damaging to his health. A former prime minister, Achille Van Acker, wrote in his memoirs that, as a bachelor, Baudouin did not know how to smile. He added that he did not learn to laugh until after his marriage.[1]

In the first years of his reign, Baudouin felt insecure, which caused him to accept the protection of the members of the government. He seldom left the royal palace and appeared infrequently in public. But the situation changed after the success of his trip to the Congo in May 1955. Four years later he visited the United States. President Eisenhower received him personally upon his arrival at the military airport in Washington.

---

1. Robert Serrou, *Balduino, El Rey* (Madrid: Palabra, 2001), 25.

Baudouin held a press conference which he handled gracefully. He traveled throughout the country for three weeks and was well accepted by the U.S. public. He returned triumphantly to Brussels. These positive experiences helped him to understand the importance of the royal function.

Later he had to confront the nationalistic tensions between the Flemish and Walloon regions of Belgium, as well as the movements for the decolonization of the Congo. In 1959 there were grave disturbances in Leopoldville, which resulted in fifty people killed and 300 wounded. The situation took the Belgians by surprise.

The king, with great realism, spoke out in favor of independence. Opposing it would not have prevented it and would have destroyed the possibility of future cooperation between the two nations.

As chief of state Baudouin maintained his distance from the internal politics of his country, taking on a role of conciliation between the different political and linguistic factions. In 1960, at the age of thirty and with almost ten years of ruling, he was very different from the awkward youth who came to the throne:

> He had learned his office by reigning. And although it was not him who had chosen that office, he showed a taste for it and real talent in representing his country abroad. He was also sensible to the great changes of history, as shown by the realism of which he showed in the matter of decolonization.[2]

The king was a bachelor without any marriage prospects, which constituted a concern for the realm. The efforts of his stepmother, Lillian of Rethy, to find a bride for him did

2. Serrou, 118.

not have positive results. Baudouin was not fond of parites or balls nor the kind of girls that frequented them, which made it much more difficult to find a suitable girl. Magazines, poorly informed, connected him to a long list of princesses.

The Search for a Bride

Bishop Leo Joseph Suenens, auxiliary to the primate of Belgium—who would become a cardinal in 1961—wrote a book in which he included his memories of meeting with Baudouin regarding his search for a bride.

Suenens first advised him to ask the help of Our Lady at the Shrine of Lourdes, where Baudouin could go incognito, mixed in with the pilgrims. The king's reply surprised him: He had recently spent a whole night praying at the grotto of the apparitions, entrusting to Our Lady the solution for his matrimonial problem. Suenens then suggested he put himself into contact with an Irish woman that he completely trusted, whom he had met in Lourdes during one of his pilgrimages. Her name was Veronica O'Brien, and she was a promoter of the Legion of Mary who had received some supernatural revelations.

Baudouin asked to meet Veronica. In an interview that lasted five hours, he confided his concern about making the right choice for a wife. Veronica thought she heard a call from the Lord inviting her to seek the solution in Catholic Spain—later she learned that this was the country the King preferred because it was Catholic; he wanted a wife who shared his faith and who, therefore, would not have to convert to Catholicism.

Veronica left in secret for Madrid carrying a letter of presentation from the king for the apostolic nuncio, which did not reveal the purpose of the visit. A friend who had a diplomatic job in Madrid counseled Veronica to have an interview with the director of a prestigious school for women in the city. During that conversation Veronica revealed the purpose of her trip, but only after obtaining a sworn promise to keep the secret. The director of the school accompanied Veronica to visit one of her alumnae. Her name was Fabiola de Mora of Aragon.

The Meeting with Fabiola de Mora of Aragon

Fabiola de Mora was born in Madrid on June 11, 1928, into an aristocratic Spanish family. She was the third daughter of Gonzalo de Mora y Fernandez Riera, the Marquis of Casa Riera, and Blanca de Aragon. Her godmother was Queen Victoria Eugenia of Spain.

During Fabiola's childhood her family resided in various European cities for political reasons. She attended primary school in Rome and in Paris. On returning to Spain she studied nursing at the Gomez Ulla Hospital of Madrid.

She was fluent in four languages. Before marrying she published a book of fairy tales, *The Twelve Amazing Tales*. When she met Fabiola, Veronica O'Brien was very struck:

> Immediately something inside told me "this is she." But common sense told me: it's impossible, given her age, she was 32. And besides, isn't she already committed? Probably. And, nevertheless, a deep part of me was convinced that I had before me the elect of Our Lady, the one who Mary herself had been preparing for a long time. . . . On seeing her room, Veronica was startled: on the wall she saw a picture that she had seen in dreams; it showed a mother with a child in her arms and there were clothes of bright red that had not yet been put away.[3]

3. Cardinal Suenens, *Balduino, El Secreto Del Rey* (Madrid: Espasa Calpe, 1995), 44–47.

Fabiola commented to Veronica that she spent many hours visiting the sick. She added that marriage was in her plans, but that her friends were much more suitable than herself, so she suggested introducing them. She was not concerned about still being without a fiancé: "I have left my life in the hands of God, I have abandoned myself to him. Perhaps He has something prepared for me."[4]

After learning the details of her visit to Spain, the king asked Veronica to go back to Madrid and invite Fabiola to spend a few days in Brussels. But Fabiola didn't trust Veronica and broke off her relationship with her. She only changed her mind when the apostolic nuncio confirmed the authenticity of Veronica's mission. Fabiola commented that the king should choose a queen of higher rank and suggested the names of several princesses. Finally she agreed to make the trip and met secretly with Baudouin at Veronica's home on the rue Suisse. Before agreeing to an engagement, Fabiola went to Lourdes to entrust her final decision to Our Lady. A few weeks later she returned to the shrine accompanied by Baudouin.

The Engagement and Wedding

On June 6, 1960, they saw each other in Lourdes at six in the evening:

> After a quick greeting, we went for a solitary walk. For close to three hours we exchanged our impressions about the situation, telling each other what had happened and what we had thought since we saw ourselves at the rue Suisse. The contact was again immediately positive, and our confidence was reciprocal: in a few minutes our friendship grew, with

---

4. Suenens, 46.

the aid of our Lady, so that, before separating on the tenth, we were able to say yes to each other.[5]

On the seventh and eighth, they returned to see each other in the crypt, attended Mass together, and continued the conversation begun on the first day. Baudouin asked Our Lady to indicate when he should declare himself. On June 9, while taking a walk, the surprise came. Baudouin told it in this way:

> Avila—Fabiola—said to me: "This time it's yes and now I will not take it back." It was too beautiful; I wanted to cry with joy and gratitude to our mother in heaven, who had done a new miracle, and to Avila, who had let herself be guided docilely by our Lady of Lourdes. It was I think, two in the afternoon and we had agreed to meet my friend and Yvette there. They saw us coming arm in arm and Avila announced that we were engaged. . . . What attracted me most in her is her humility, her trust in the Blessed Virgin, and her transparency. I know that she has always been for me a great stimulus to love God more each day.[6]

On August 15, 1960, Fabiola took advantage of the fact that her whole family was gathered at their summer villa in Zarauz, near San Sebastian, to announce her decision at the moment when photos were being taken: "This is my last photo as a single. My fiancé's name is Baudouin. He is the king of the Belgians."

Gaston Eyskens, Belgium's prime minister, interrupted a radio program to announce the engagement of the king and Fabiola. When the Belgians learned that the king had chosen a Spanish wife, they were somewhat taken aback. They had

---

5. Suenens, 55.
6. Suenens, 56–58.

not forgotten that four centuries earlier, Philip II had sent the cruel Duke of Alba to extirpate Protestantism in their country by force. He had executed the Counts Hoorn and Egmont, two legendary heroes. The Belgians' lack of confidence toward the betrothed who where Catholic and unknown ended when they learned it was a marriage of love not convenience and when they saw how happy the king was at her side.

On September 13 Fabiola traveled by automobile, driven by a chauffeur, from Zarauz to Belgium, accompanied by her mother and her brother Gonzalo. After spending a night in Paris, they reached the palace of Ciergnon, where Baudouin awaited them. From there they went to the royal palace of Brussels, where they were acclaimed by the multitude. On the eve of their wedding, they were given a gala meal in the royal palace.

September 15 was an historic day for the Belgians. The religious ceremony was celebrated in the Cathedral of St. Michael and St. Gudula. The dignitaries of the kingdom were there. Eight thousand people were invited. At twelve thirty the couple entered the church. Contrary to custom, it was Baudouin who accompanied his betrothed by his express desire. Cardinal Van Roey waited for him in the sanctuary, assisted by Bishop Suenens. Veronica was not present; she preferred to follow the ceremony by television. Fabiola sent her a friendly message of gratitude: "Till now I knew that Our Lady was the queen and mother and that she also had many other attributions, but I did not know that she was also the organizer of marriages."

Upon leaving the cathedral there was a hundred-gun salute, and five thousand doves were released. Baudouin and Fabiola greeted the crowds that had gathered. On the afternoon of their wedding, they traveled by plane to Seville, and from there they went to Calixto, an estate provided by the Marquis of Salinas, Fabiola's brother. They had to interrupt their honeymoon because of a strike in Brussels, the result of the economic crisis in the country.

On their return to the palace, they encountered a disagreeable surprise: The former King Leopold and Queen Lillian, Baudouin's stepmother, had all the palace furniture moved to the Argenteuil palace, their new residence. From that moment the relationship between the two couples became quite cool.

Baudouin and Fabiola's Married Life

On June 8, 1961, six months after their marriage, the king and queen were received by John XXIII. They informed the pope that they were expecting a child before announcing it to the Belgians. On their return from the trip, the queen felt ill. It was her first miscarriage. In 1962 and 1963 she suffered two more miscarriages.

For many years they maintained the hope of having children, until, finally, they accepted that it was not possible. The queen admitted that she had suffered five miscarriages, but that she had learned to live with this. The king spoke before seven hundred children that were visiting Laeken Palace. "We have asked ourselves the meaning of this suffering: little by little we have understood that our heart is thus freer to love all children, absolutely all."

Cardinal Suenens asked himself, in the biography he wrote, what the king's secret was. And he gave the following answer:

> One does not have to look far: it was to be found in the depth of his spiritual life. In other words, in his union with God, lived as a Christian, day by day, and translated into daily gestures of service to others.[7]

---

7. Suenens, 77.

Baudouin renounced his functions as chief of state for forty-four hours between the April 3 and April 5, 1990, in opposition to the law legalizing abortion and to avoid having to approve it. He did this because the law was opposed to the right to life and it clashed with his Catholic beliefs, even though he ran the risk that Parliament would not approve his return to power.

At the age of sixty-three, Baudouin felt tired and sick. On July 23, 1993, he sent a letter to his friend Cardinal Suenens admitting his weakness in performing his daily tasks. He was suffering, but he did not forget others who also suffered and whom he visited. He asked God's help each day to be able to suffer with joy as the saints did.

His last official address to the country was on July 21, 1993. It had the importance of a testament. Later he left to spend a few days resting with Fabiola at his summer residence of Villa Astrida, in Motril, a beautiful village of Granada.

Baudouin Dies Suddenly

On July 31, the queen called the king to dinner several times without getting an answer. She found her husband seated in an armchair on the terrace with the book he had been reading on the floor. She quickly called Carlos Aguarda, a cardiac specialist, who tried in vain to resuscitate the monarch. He had died of a heart attack. His remains were flown to Laeken Palace. In his hands was the "fiat rosary" he liked so much.

His first wake was held in the palace chapel, where Fabiola prayed alone. Later there was a public wake in the royal palace with the king dressed in his military uniform. Next to the coffin was a bouquet of white roses with the inscription "To my heart, Fabiola."

The funeral was broadcast by Eurovision. Queen Fabiola personally chose the music. Dressed in white, she wanted the sorrow to be transformed into a day of glory and hope. The liturgy proclaimed the victory of life over death. In his homily Cardinal Danneels spoke of how the king confronted the suffering that never left him in a Christian way. There was also a reference to his wife:

> This man, filled with love, had to be a model in his marriage and family life. In the Queen he has left us what is probably the most valuable of his legacies. Beyond death, which has scarcely separated them, the King and Queen really have the right to tell us: We ask you then to imitate us.[8]

Baudouin was buried in the royal crypt of the Church of Our Lady of Laeken. Fabiola received some 300,000 letters of condolence. Some of them asked that Baudouin be declared a saint. Since Baudouin did not have any children, the throne passed to his brother Alberto, Prince of Liege, married to Princess Paola Ruffo di Calabria. After the death of her husband, Queen Fabiola dedicated herself to works of charity and continued as head of the King Baudouin Foundation, created in 1976 to combat poverty, promote ecology, and help the Third World.

■ ■ ■

A Marriage that Remained Ever Young

As the years passed, Baudouin and Fabiola proved they were made for each other. In the king's spiritual diary, there are frequent mentions of a married love that did not fall into mere

---

8. Suenens, 159–161.

habit but remained as vivid and young as in the first days. On each anniversary of the day of their engagement, the king renewed his thanksgiving to God for that encounter. In a note dated July 8, 1978, Baudouin wrote:

> It is eighteen years since Fabiola and I gave our word to one another, on leaving Mass on the feast of St. Elisabeth of Portugal, in Lourdes. Thank you, O Lord, for having led us by the hand to the feet of Mary, and from then on, every day. Thank you, O Lord, for having loved us in your love and for having increased in this love day by day.[9]

They never took their mutual love for granted. They knew that love either grows or dies. Throughout their long married life, they never took time off: the romantic conquest of their courting stage was never interrupted. They were always open to loving more and better, knowing that married love is built every day through small sacrifices and concessions, with small details that brighten the life of the other, and with forgiveness granted again and again.

Marital harmony is the result of practicing many virtues: sincerity, respect, understanding, patience, and so on, but when these are lacking, there is another recourse that never fails: to have a "poor memory." The secret of many happy marriages is never keeping a list of grievances. One has to know how to forgive and forget again and again.

Marriage as a Vocation

For Baudouin and Fabiola marriage was not simply a vital option; it was a human and supernatural vocation.

---

9. Suenens, 61.

Marriage as a sacrament is not a substitute for marriage as a natural contract, given that both have the same ends and properties. It is a natural and supernatural reality at the same time:

> The sacramental character of marriage does not make married love lose any of its human aspects. It is that very natural law itself born between a man and a woman with its character of affection, of feeling, of aspiration to be no more than one heart and one soul, with its bodily attraction and desire to love each other, which is elevated by Christ to a sacrament; a reality which is a fount of sanctification and salvation. Christ made use of spousal love to make known what the love is like with which he loves the Church, and, therefore, married love should be a reflection of that love.[10]

Baudouin and Fabiola lived their marriage as an alliance of love between them and with God. Marriage was a path to sanctity for both of them. They sanctified themselves by fulfilling with perfection their duties as wife and husband. The grace of the sacrament strengthened them to maintain a love of total self-giving in all the circumstances of their life, including the most difficult and painful. It also helped them to grow in supernatural charity. Baudouin loved Fabiola—not *for* love of God but *with* the love of God:

> Almost every day I see in my life palpable signs of the love of God. Fabiola has been and continues to be one of the most outstanding. Sometimes—few—I have asked myself if all of this is not too wonderful to be true, and if it is not a fruit of my imagination, like a fairy tale that no one has to see as hard reality.[11]

---

10. Amadeo Aparicio, *El Matrimonio a Examen* (Pamplona: EUNSA, 2003), 225.
11. Suenens, 78.

United by Forgetfulness of Self and Shared Suffering

The absence of children not only did not separate Baudouin and Fabiola, it was a stimulus for them to remain united. They jointly accepted the suffering caused by this. On December 14, 1990, after thirty years of marriage, the queen expressed her feelings in a televised message:

> I would say simply that they have been years of happiness, due on the one hand to the loveableness of my husband, to his attentions, to a constant self-forgetfulness that never failed. I don't say this lightly, for he has had patience with me through everything: this is why our love has increased and has always provided fresh flowers. That forgetfulness of oneself in favor of the other, is really the key to a happy marriage. For love and happiness are one and the same, which does not exclude suffering. The very sharing of difficulties consolidates love. At the heart of every suffering there is a promise of life, like in the spring.[12]

Married love has an order: The other spouse comes first. One has to live more for the other than for oneself, avoiding the egoism of a possessive love, which only leads to failure. If one thinks of oneself too much, one stops thinking of the other person and of ways to make them happy—to make someone else happy it's necessary to forget about oneself. Not only does this not harm one's own happiness but rather increases it; happiness is not attained directly, but as a result of making the person one loves happy. In marriage the happiness of each spouse depends on that of the other. There is one law that is always fulfilled: Either both are happy or neither.

---

12. Serrou, 140.

The self-forgetfulness that Fabiola spoke of in 1990 was lived by her in a very special way three years later, when Baudouin became gravely ill. She comforted him with her sympathetic company and with her loving, tender care:

> Fabiola did all that was possible to see that he unwind, and rest, in that abode surrounded by palm trees, oleanders and orange trees, and whose view extended over the light blue waters of the Mediterranean. In the evening it would be the Queen herself who would do the cooking and, when everything was ready, call the King to supper, together in all simplicity. As they both liked to do, with their two dachshunds, Miko and Toffec, as their only witnesses.[13]

The sudden and unexpected death of Baudouin interrupted a long love story, but at the same time it underlined the beauty it contained:

> At that moment there began a long and sorrowful night for the Queen, which saw brutally interrupted a great romance of love that had begun thirty-three years earlier. A legendary love that defied the laws of time. Thirty-three years during which, together, inseparable in pomp and in sorrow, they had fought for the most varied causes, without ever failing to bring a witness of compassion and human warmth to all those who suddenly found themselves afflicted by fate.[14]

---

13. Serrou, 201.
14. Serrou, 202.